CW00407639

Twice in a Lifetime

A musical

Story and Book by Ray Cooney

Music by
Chris Walker and Keith Strachan

Property of
alra Academy of Live
& Recorded Arts
DO NOT REMOVE FROM LIBRARY
020 8870 6475 | info@alra.co.uk

Samuel French — London
www.samuelfrench-london.co.uk

© 2010 BY RAY COONEY PRODUCTIONS LTD

This play is fully protected under the Copyright Laws of the British Commonwealth of Nations, the United States of America and all countries of the Berne and Universal Copyright Conventions.

All rights including Stage, Motion Picture, Radio, Television, Public Reading, and Translation into Foreign Languages, are strictly reserved.

No part of this publication may lawfully be reproduced in ANY form or by any means—photocopying, typescript, recording (including video-recording), manuscript, electronic, mechanical, or otherwise—or be transmitted or stored in a retrieval system, without prior permission.

SAMUEL FRENCH LTD, 52 FITZROY STREET, LONDON W1T 5JR or their authorized agents, issue licences to amateurs to give performances of this play on payment of a fee. **This fee is subject to contract and subject to variation at the sole discretion of Samuel French Ltd.**

Licences for amateur performances are issued subject to the understanding that it shall be made clear in all advertising matter that the audience will witness an amateur performance; that the names of the authors of the plays shall be included on all programmes; and that the integrity of the authors' work will be preserved.

Amateur Rights are controlled in the USA and Canada by SAMUEL FRENCH INC., 45 West 25th Street, New York, NY 10010, USA.

The publication of this play does not imply that it is necessarily available for performance by amateurs or professionals, either in the British Isles or Overseas. Amateurs and professionals considering a production are strongly advised in their own interests to apply to the appropriate agents for consent before starting rehearsals or booking a theatre or hall.

The right of Ray Cooney be identified as author of the book and Chris Walker and Keith Strachan to be identified as composers of the music of this work has been asserted by them in accordance with Section 77 of the Copyright, Designs and Patents Act 1988

ISBN 978 0 573 18042 2

TWICE IN A LIFETIME

CAST LIST: (in order of appearance)

Johnny May, a young man in his twenties
Fingers, a weasly-looking gangster
Steven Tancred, a young man in his twenties
Dr Patel, an Asian Hypnotherapist aged 30-50
Mr Gregory Pilsworth, the domineering boss of a law firm
Jeff Walters, a dedicated lawyer full of charm. In his thirties
Barbara Pilsworth, a stern but sexy lawyer
Miss Dixon, a young but frumpy secretary
Bugs Moran, a hard-nosed man in his fifties
Ruby, a tough but, underneath, vulnerable girl
Arnold Robertson, a ruthless property developer
Mrs Daphne Pilsworth, a silly woman in her late fifties
Mrs Emily Clarke, a cheerful and feisty lady. Any age between 75 and 90
Linda Clarke, an independent gutsy young girl in her twenties
Vicar, a nervous man of indeterminate age

SUBSIDIARY ROLES

ACT I	ACT II
Cop	Foreman
Two Floozies	Workmen
Barber	1st "Cop"
Customers	Police Sergeant: Capone
1929 Characters	Young Cop
"Today" Office Staff	Other Cop
Two Gangsters: Frankie	Mrs Barber
& Sammy	Two Bridesmaids
Waiter	
Night Club Customers	
Young Bum	
Dr Patel's Receptionist	
Catering Manager	
Three Happy Couples	

COPYRIGHT INFORMATION

(See also page ii)

This play is fully protected under the Copyright Laws of the British Commonwealth of Nations, the United States of America and all countries of the Berne and Universal Copyright Conventions.
All rights including Stage, Motion Picture, Radio, Television, Public Reading, and Translation into Foreign Languages, are strictly reserved.

No part of this publication may lawfully be reproduced in ANY form or by any means — photocopying, typescript, recording (including video-recording), manuscript, electronic, mechanical, or otherwise—or be transmitted or stored in a retrieval system, without prior permission.

Licences for amateur performances are issued subject to the understanding that it shall be made clear in all advertising matter that the audience will witness an amateur performance; that the names of the authors of the plays shall be included on all programmes; and that the integrity of the authors' work will be preserved.

The Royalty Fee is subject to contract and subject to variation at the sole discretion of Samuel French Ltd.

In Theatres or Halls seating Four Hundred or more the fee will be subject to negotiation.

In Territories Overseas the fee quoted above may not apply. A fee will be quoted on application to our local authorized agent, or if there is no such agent, on application to Samuel French Ltd, London.

VIDEO-RECORDING OF AMATEUR PRODUCTIONS

Please note that the copyright laws governing video-recording are extremely complex and that it should not be assumed that any play may be video-recorded for whatever purpose without first obtaining the permission of the appropriate agents. The fact that a play is published by Samuel French Ltd does not indicate that video rights are available or that Samuel French Ltd controls such rights.

SYNOPSIS OF SCENES

ACT I

ACT II

Running time - about 2 hours 30 minutes including interval

MUSICAL NUMBERS

ACT I

No. 1	Rat-a-Tat Rag	Everyone
No. 2	The Monday Morning Meeting	Steven, Mr Pilsworth, Jeff, Barbara and Staff
No. 3	The Monday Morning Meeting (reprise)	Steven, Mr Pilsworth, Jeff, Barbara and Staff
No. 4	You're Gonna Love Chicago	Johnny, Fingers, Bugs, Ruby and Gangsters
No. 5	One of Those Moments	Johnny and Ruby
No. 6	The Thing About Ruby	Steven
No. 7	Rat-a-Tat Rag	Bugs, Fingers and Gangsters
No. 8	He's Having an Affair	Barbara, Mrs Pilsworth, Manager and Happy Couples
No. 9	Deep in My Heart	Ruby
No. 10	The Best is Yet to Come	Everyone

ACT II

No. 11	In the Rain	Mrs Clarke, Jeff and Builders
No. 12	The Hit	Jeff, Steven and Chicagoans
No. 13	Trust Me	Linda and Steven
No. 14	Time's Up	Jeff, Barbara, Mr Pilsworth, Johnny, Bugs, and Ensemble
No. 15	One of Those Moments (reprise)	Johnny and Ruby
No. 16	This Can't Be Right	Linda and Steven
No. 17	The Thing About Ruby (reprise)	Linda
No. 18	Move It	Linda, Steven, Jeff
No. 19	Rat-a-Tat Rag (reprise)	Al and Cop
No. 20	Tell Him	Linda, Barbara, Mr Pilsworth and Congregation
No. 21	Two of Those Moments	Full Company

The piano/vocal score is available on hire from:
SAMUEL FRENCH LTD, 52 FITZROY STREET, LONDON W1T 5JR

AUTHOR'S NOTE

At the time of "going to print" we have done four workshops (of varying degrees of sophistication!) and one full-scale "try-out" production at the Yvonne Arnaud Theatre, Guildford and another full-scale "try-out" in Los Angeles. We have learnt a lot!

Firstly, "Twice in a Lifetime" appears to be a real "Audience Pleaser". Secondly, it is extremely complicated. In addition, it can be staged either simply (in a small village hall with no sets and a piano) or with a £5,000,000 budget at Drury Lane with state-of-the-art back projection and a 25-piece orchestra.

However, what is unavoidable is the size of the Cast. Eleven principals and twelve (settle for ten!) ensemble is ideal – although with a lot of "doubling" and "gender-bending" (female to male), it could be done with eight (settle for six!) ensemble. To that end, for instance, you would need "The Young Bum" to be played by one of the female ensemble members and for the actors playing Jeff and Mr Pilsworth to double as American Cops. One could certainly use the actors playing Mr and Mrs Pilsworth, Miss Clarke and Miss Dixon and Jeff as "Customers" in the 1929 Nightclub scene.

The size of the band is obviously dictated by the budget, but, in Guildford, we found that six (with the MD doubling on keyboard) serves the show well. In Los Angeles we had ten which was great!

The "simpler" the set is, we feel, the better, with the costumes, lighting and sound giving the "theatrical" feel to the production.

The quicker one moves to and from the TODAY scenes to 1929 the better. Hence we suggest (as indicated in the script) that Steven simply walks from TODAY into the 1929 scenes rather than trying to do tricksey stuff with doubles.

To revert to the Set for a moment. If the budget can afford it, a raised platform, say 8ft high, running across backstage from L to R is most useful. At Guildford and Los Angeles we used it very effectively in those scenes that combined TODAY and 1929 with the 1929 characters appearing on the platform. In various other scenes it came in very handy e.g. the scaffolding in ACT II, Scene 1. Apart from that we just used three wing-pieces L and R for entrances and exits. All members of the cast assisted in bringing on furniture, props etc.

Most of the time the artistes will have time to change costumes from 1929 to TODAY – well most of the time! "Steven" always stays in present-day costume as "Johnny" except for Johnny wearing a 1929 hat and coat for his first entrance which he "loses" as he walks into TODAY.

Those actors who "inadvertently" regress Steven, must make sure that they replicate the same "to and fro" movement across Steven's eyes as Dr Patel's pendant. You will, we think, be pleasantly surprised at how quickly and enthusiastically the audiences respond to this! The actors who accidentally regress Steven must always remember to continue to address Steven in the position he was in even though Steven has walked out of the scene.

We're probably teaching the directors and actors to "suck eggs" but, in "singing" the numbers, don't forget the "acting" side of it. Keep the dramatic line going through the lyrics – i.e. Don't just sing!

Lastly – ENJOY. We think you'll find it a fun piece. And, remember – team work! You need each other! Huge good luck with our musical. We've loved it.

Ray Cooney

ACT I

Before the CURTAIN *rises we hear eerie 1920's style music: Rat-a-Tat Rag*

No. 1 Rat-a-Tat Rag

The CURTAIN *rises*

SCENE 1

A Chicago Street. Night. 1929

The eerie music continues underneath the scene

The Lights come up on a Chicago street. It is cold and snowing. Chicagoans are hurrying to and fro. A policeman ambles by swinging his truncheon. At the rear of the set is a row of shops, one of which is a barber shop. Through the window of the shop we see two men being shaved by the barbers. They are talking and joking

After a few moments Johnny May, a fresh-faced young man in his twenties, enters from DR *nervously smoking a cigarette and looks around apprehensively. He is wearing a 1929 overcoat and hat. He stands there, watching until the street is clear*

Johnny Yeah. Yeah. It's all clear, Fingers!

Fingers, a weasly-looking gangster, enters. He wears spectacles and conceals a tommy-gun

Fingers OK kid, get back in the car.
Johnny What you gonna do, Fingers? What's the plan?
Fingers Shut up. In the car! Behind the wheel!
Johnny Yeah but what you gonna do?
Fingers Get in the car! (*He hits Johnny across the shoulder and moves upstage*)

*After a moment Fingers takes out a tommy-gun and enters the shop. The
two barbers step back in horror. Fingers lets loose with his tommy-gun.
Two men writhe in agony for several seconds before slumping in their
chairs as the white towels covering them turn red with blood. Fingers
runs out of the shop*

*During the shooting Johnny has covered his ears and reacted in horror
but is unable to take his eyes off the gruesome murder*

Johnny! Get back in the car!

Johnny is staring at the scene speechless

Johnny May! Get in the car! (*He slaps Johnny hard across the
shoulder*)
Johnny (*yelling*) Ahhh!

Light effects and the music becomes very loud

(*Echoing*) Ahhhhhhh!!

The set becomes

SCENE 2

Dr Patel's Consulting Room. Present Day

*The small room is DL with a door leading into the corridor in the ULC
wall. Ragtime music discordantly segues into transcendental music.
Johnny, losing his overcoat and hat on the way, walks stage L into the
set, lays back on the couch and "becomes" Steven. Dr Patel is sitting
beside him. Dr Patel is holding his pendant. Steven's jacket is hanging
on the back of the couch. Steven is wearing shirt and tie*

Johnny (*off; continuing*) Ahhhhh!
Steven (*sitting up*) Ahhh!
Dr Patel (*standing up and moving down to Steven's L; soothingly*) It's
all right, Steven, it's all right.
Steven (*looking around bewildered; being scared and confused*) That
was scary. That was really — frightening. I was in America — in
Chicago — with a chap called Fingers.
Dr Patel (*smiling*) Well, you're safely back in England now — in

Putney — with a chap called Dr Patel. Now take some deep breaths. (*He lays Steven back*)

Steven (*sitting up*) It was like something out of a Humphrey Bogart movie!

Dr Patel Humphrey Bogart movies, I love them! (*Laying Steven back and waving the pendant to and fro as he speaks*) Just relax — watch the pendant and listen to my voice.

Steven (*sitting up*) I only came here to quit smoking you know!

Dr Patel (*laying Steven back and swinging the pendant as he speaks*) Mr Tancred you came to a hypnotherapist to assist you in regard to your nicotine addiction, but sometimes, in a hypnotic state — in a trance — the subject is — inadvertently — momentarily — regressed...

Steven (*sitting up*) Regressed?

Dr Patel Taken back to a previous life.

Steven Are you telling me I was once a gangster?

Dr Patel Why not?

Steven That's great for a lawyer.

Dr Patel Mr Tancred, if you have regressed to an earlier existence maybe it's because you need to learn something from that person — in order to improve your life today.

Steven My life's almost perfect!

Dr Patel (*smiling*) You said "almost".

Steven It's practically perfect.

Dr Patel (*smiling*) Practically? Now lay back. (*Laying Steven back and swings the pendant to and fro as he speaks*) For a moment your subconscious may take over. All perfectly normal.

Steven (*sitting up*) Normal?! (*Standing up and grabbing his jacket*) Excuse me, I have to drive to Windsor. It's the Monday morning meeting. Busy, busy, busy! (*He hurries out of the door of Dr Patel's office*)

SCENE 3

The Offices of Pilsworth And Pilsworth And Co. Present Day

No. 2 The Monday Morning Meeting

Staff   Busy, busy, busy, busy, busy,
                             Busy, busy, busy, busy, busy

During the above the office staff have appeared from all directions including along the upstage platform, hurrying to the meeting

Mr Pilsworth hurries on DL *followed by Miss Dixon who is busily attempting to take Mr Pilsworth's notes*

Mr Pilsworth (*to the audience*) It's the Monday morning meeting
I've no time to indulge
In a lot of idle chit-chat
I've something to divulge
To the whole of the department
At ten precisely whence
The Monday morning meeting will commence.

He hurries out UR

Miss Dixon (*to audience*) I don't know how we'll
Handle the suspense!

She hurries after Mr Pilsworth

An agitated Steven is pushed on by a tense Jeff from DL *and marched across the stage. Steven is smoking a cigarette*

Steve (*turning as he's pushed; speaking*) I tell you, Jeff, it was nineteen twenty-nine! These guys had tommy-guns. There was blood flying everywhere — it was terrifying! Madness!

Jeff (*singing*)   It's the Monday morning meeting
You've no time to engage
In a lot of utter drivel
So try to act your age
Mr Pilsworth will be waiting
With a comprehensive list
So no more talk of things
That don't exist
Or everyone will think that
You are pi——
(*He is interrupted by some of the staff and Miss Dixon as she is hurrying them to the meeting*)
Staff   Busy! Busy! Busy!
Here at Pilsworth and Co.
Legally we're very in the know

We'll help you plead/draw up a deed
A contract or a will.

Miss Dixon   If you're rich enough to pay our bill

The Staff and Miss Dixon exit

Barbara enters from DR *dragging an even more agitated Steven across the stage to* DL

Barbara I told you not to visit that quack!
Steven (*stopping*) Darling, listen! I was regressed! I was Johnny May!
A Chicago gangster!

Barbara (*grabbing the cigarette from him; singing*)
It's the Monday morning meeting
Ignore this Johnny May
And forget about the twenties
Just focus on today
It's the Monday morning meeting
With Daddy in the chair
So unless you want to find a job elsewhere
Just give a smile and
Comment on my hair (*She goes to pull him*
DL)

Steven (*speaking; resisting*) I need a cigarette!

Steven rushes off DR

Barbara (*yelling after him*) Steven! (*Looking at her watch; furiously*)
Oo!

She hurries off DL

During the following Mr Pilsworth's magnificent desk moves from UC *to* DC *with Mr Pilsworth sitting behind it opening letters with his gold-plated letter-opener. Miss Dixon sits in her chair beside the desk poised to take notes. As they sing the Staff march in from all directions and assemble* DL *for the meeting*

Staff (*singing*)   We're busy! Busy! Busy!
Here at Pilsworth and Co.

Mr Pilsworth keeps us on the go
We're busy! Busy! Busy!
Endeavouring to please.
Miss Dixon (*to audience*) And collecting those outrageous fees.

During the following Barbara hurries in from UL *as Jeff hurries in from* DR, *they meet* DR *with Barbara on Jeff's* L. *In furious dumb-show Jeff asks Barbara where Steven is. Barbara, even more furious, mimes smoking a cigarette*

Staff   Busy! Busy! Busy! Busy!
                                    Busy! Busy! Busy! Busy!
                                    Busy! Busy! Busy!
                                    Here at Pilsworth and Co.

As Barbara is furiously miming cigarette smoking Mr Pilsworth looks up. Barbara and Jeff immediately give Mr Pilsworth a huge innocent smile. Mr Pilsworth looks at his watch then looks at Miss Dixon

Mr Pilsworth (*speaking*) Time?!
Miss Dixon (*looking at her watch*) Ten a.m. — and thirty-seven seconds.
Mr Pilsworth (*singing*) It's the Monday morning meeting
                                    And ev'rybody's here
                                    Excepting Mr Tancred
                                    Whose lack of zeal is clear
                                    It's the Monday morning meeting
                                    I'm ready to commence
                                    And Tancred has to keep us in suspense.
Miss Dixon (*to audience*) I only hope he has a good defence.

A disturbed Steven hurriedly tip-toes in from UL

The Staff giggle at Steven's entrance

Mr Pilsworth hurriedly turns to look at the Staff — by which time Steven has tip-toed behind Mr Pilsworth and stands beside Barbara on her L. *Mr Pilsworth turns to Miss Dixon*

Mr Pilsworth In the minutes! Mr Tancred late for the Monday morning — (*He stops and does a "double take" on seeing Steven standing beside Barbara*)

Steven tries to smile and gives a weak wave of his hand

Explain yourself, Mr Tancred!
Steven (*emotionally, in one breath*) I'm terribly sorry, sir, but I've had the most terrifying experience in Chicago in nineteen twenty-nine with a frightful person called Fingers who massacred these two chaps in front of my very eyes. (*Miming*) Rat-tat-tat-tat-tat-tat-tat-tat-tat.

Pause. Then one of the female staff emits a silly giggle. Mr Pilsworth glares at her — she stops. Mr Pilsworth looks back at Steven

(*Hoarsely*) I was regressed to being Johnny May.
Mr Pilsworth (*ominously*) You were — "regressed"?

Miss Dixon (*singing*)	Who'd have thought it, Mr Pilsworth?
Jeff (*stepping in*)	But he fought it, Mr Pilsworth.
Steven	These guys were at the barbers
	When they bought it, Mr Pilsworth
	They went and died
	I nearly cried
	I really was upset.
Barbara (*stepping in*)	Please, Daddy darling — don't fret.

Mr Pilsworth (*giving them an icy glare*; *deadpan*) Right. We have two items on this morning's agenda. (*He flicks his fingers towards Miss Dixon*)
Miss Dixon (*reading*) Item one. "Smoking".
Mr Pilsworth (*ominously*) Yes, smoking! How many of you have abandoned this filthy habit?

All the staff shoot their hands up — except Steven. Mr Pilsworth glares at Steven who half-heartedly puts his hand up

Steven I'm down to twenty a day.
Mr Pilsworth Twenty?! I said — (*rising and menacingly approaching Steven*)

(*Singing*)	No smoking, Mr Tancred.
Jeff (*singing*)	No joking, Mr Tancred.
Mr Pilsworth	Or soon you could be working in Woking,
	Mr Tancred
Barbara ⎱ (*together*)	You really must give up or bust
Jeff ⎰	This time you have to quit

All (*except Steven*)   Or Mr Tancred — that's it!

Steven Well, that's why I went to see Dr Patel and ——
Mr Pilsworth (*interrupting*) Forget Dr Patel. The trick is to keep busy,
   Tancred.

All (*except Steven*) Busy!
Steven   Who sir?
All (*except Steven*) Busy!
Mr Pilsworth   You, sir
All (*except Steven*) Busy!
Mr Pilsworth   As a ——
All (*except Steven*) Busy!
Mr Pilsworth   — bee, sir!
All (*except Steven*) Busy!
Steven   Me, sir?
All (*except Steven*) Busy!
Mr Pilsworth   Here at Pilsworth and Co.

*During the following the Staff advance on Steven. they get increasingly
angry with Steven as he mimes all the "horror" of his 1929 experience*

Steven (*even more distressed*)   **Staff** We're busy! Busy! Busy!
   Couldn't sort it,   Here at Pilsworth
   Mr Pilsworth   And Co.
   Or thwart it,   That's what
   Mr Pilsworth   Mr Pilsworth likes
   These guys were at the barbers   You know
   When they bought it,   We're busy! Busy! Busy!
   Mr Pilsworth   That's what we're paid to be
   They went and died   So forget Chicago
   I nearly cried   Q.E.D.
   I really was upset
   Don't think I'll ever forget

   Mr Pilsworth ⎫   No smoking, Mr Tancred
   Jeff   ⎬ (*together*) No joking, Mr Tancred
   Barbara   ⎭   Or soon you could be working
                                                      In Woking, Mr Tancred
                                                      You really must give up or bust
                                                      This time you have to quit
                                                      Or Mr Tancred – that's it.

Jeff stops Steven singing by putting his hand over Steven's mouth and Barbara stops the miming by fiercely wrapping her arms around him

Staff	We're busy, so busy
Mr Pilsworth	And that's the end of item one!
All (*splitting*)	Item one! Item one! Item one! Item one!

End of number

Mr Pilsworth Staff, positions!

The Staff return to their regimental group DL *and Mr Pilsworth to his desk*

So, with Mr Tancred's permission we'll move on to *item two*. (*He looks at Miss Dixon*)

Miss Dixon (*reading*) Mr Arnold Robertson!

Mr Pilsworth Yes! (*Picking up a file*) Mr Robertson is the most significant property developer in South East England and Pilsworth and Pilsworth are representing his interests in relation to a certain Mrs Emily Beatrice Clarke. I've decided to place this vital matter in the joint hands of Mr Walters and Mr Tancred.

There is applause from the Staff as all except Steven look delighted. Barbara kisses Steven

(*To Staff*) Stop that! Mr Robertson is due at ten fifteen for an initial meeting with Mr Walters and Mr Tancred so — Meeting closed! No problems! Busy, Busy, Busy!

The Staff start to disperse and Staff start to sing

No. 2a Busy Cues

Staff (*singing*)	Busy,
	Busy,
	Busy, busy, busy,
	Busy,
	Busy ——

Steven (*interrupting; speaking*) I — think — there — could be a slight problem, Mr Pilsworth.

Musical punctuation. The Staff all stop and turn

Mr Pilsworth (*looking up*) You're not going to be your usual pain in the arse, are you, Steven?
Steven (*cheerfully*) I probably am, sir, yes.
Jeff (*aside to Barbara*) Here we go!
Miss Dixon Excuse me, Mr Pilsworth, shall I re-word "pain in the arse"?
Mr Pilsworth No!
Steven Well, you see, Sir, according to the correspondence, I've seen Mrs Clarke has lived in her little cottage just outside Windsor since the nineteen fifties and now, with her husband gone, she just wants to die there.
Mr Pilsworth Well Steven, according to the correspondence, *I've* seen, everybody concerned in the village of Datchet has accepted Mr Robertson's generous financial offer for their properties except this obstinate old bat whose wretched cottage is standing slap bang in the middle of his fifteen million pound half-completed shopping centre!
Steven I'm afraid you're missing the point, sir.
Mr Pilsworth No Steven, *you're* missing the point! Mr Robertson intends to open his shopping mall by Christmas which can only be achieved by somehow getting Mrs Clarke O-U-T and demolishing her C-O-T-T-A-G-E. So, meeting closed. Busy, busy, busy!

The Staff start to disperse

Staff (*singing*) Busy! Busy!
                        Busy, busy, busy! ——
Steven (*interrupting*; *singing*) I hadn't quite finished, Mr Pilsworth!

Mr Pilsworth furiously bangs his letter-opener on the desk as the Staff freeze

Mr Pilsworth Why the hell do I put up with you, Steven?
Steven (*politely*) It's probably because I'm engaged to your daughter and she finds me rather sexy.

Mr Pilsworth is left open-mouthed. The girls giggle

Mr Pilsworth Stop that! Steven! Mr Robertson is paying our company a small fortune to get Mrs Clarke O-U-T so you and Mr Walters will devise a method — (*He looks at Staff*)

Staff To get Mrs Clarke O-U-T.
   (*Starting to disperse*; *singing*)   Busy!
                                        Busy——
Steven (*interrupting*; *speaking*) It's a question of ethics, morals, decency!

The Staff freeze

Mr Pilsworth (*almost choking as he speaks*) Ethics, morals, decency?!
We're *lawyers*, Mr Tancred, we deal with the *law*.

No. 3 Monday Morning Meeting (Reprise)

Mr Pilsworth	When this firm was founded
	Back in nineteen-oh-five
	My father's father taught him how to thrive
	If your client is a saint or sinner
	Isn't your concern
	Just as long as he's got cash to burn
Steven	Money can't buy everything, Mr —
Mr Pilsworth	That's a lesson you have yet to learn
Staff	Keep learning
Mr Pilsworth	Keep earning
	See Missus Clarke gets O-U-T
	Or very soon you'll be job free

Steven (*speaking*) But, it's just not right —

During the final bars of the Number the ensemble lift Mr Pilsworth onto their shoulders and he adopts a Caesar-like pose

Mr Pilsworth   You will be out of work my friend
Steven (*speaking*) Just give me two minutes!
Mr Pilsworth   I think this meeting's at an end
All   At an end
                        At an end
                        At an end
                        At an end

With the music playing underneath the Staff march off carrying Mr Pilsworth with Barbara and Jeff bringing up the rear

End of reprise

Steven (*dejected; watches for a moment then hurries after them*) Mr
Pilsworth I wish to register my very strong objections to — !

*Steven exits after them but immediately returns being "frog-marched"
by Jeff and Barbara*

Jeff What the hell's the matter with you?
Barbara Yes, what the hell's the matter, darling?!
Steven Listen, what with Dr Patel and your father I've had a very
disturbing morning and I need to sort myself out.
Jeff You need to sort out Mrs Clarke, that's all!
Barbara Yes, sort out Mrs Clarke, darling.
Steven What we're being asked to do to that old lady is not right!!
Jeff Just shut your eyes and think of the bonus!
Barbara Think of the bonus!
Jeff Trade in the Ford Focus for a BMW!
Barbara Down payment on a house!
Jeff Trust fund for those kids you're going to have!
Barbara Our babies!
Steven I have to live with myself.
Jeff (*pointedly*) You have to live with Barbara too.
Barbara (*coyly*) For ever and ever. (*Looking at watch*) Due in court.
(*Suddenly serious*) Don't spoil everything darling. We're getting
married next month. Everything's almost perfect.
Steven (*smiling wryly*) Almost perfect.
Barbara Yeah, great! See you! (*She kisses Steven*)

Barbara hurries out DR

Jeff That is one hell of a sexy lady.
Steven (*smiling*) Almost perfect.

Mr Pilsworth hurries in from DL

Mr Pilsworth Right! Mr Robertson has arrived. Have you pulled
yourself together, Steven?
Steven Mr Pilsworth, I'm sorry but the Mrs Clarkes of this world should
be protected not persecuted.
Mr Pilsworth Steven!

Music **No. 3a**

(*Starting to flick his letter-opener in front of Steven's face to make his points*) This wretched woman has refused all Mr Robertson's offers to buy so he wants her O-U-T. So we will get her O-U-T. O-K?!

During the above speech Steven's eyes have been going from side to side and he is starting to be hypnotised by the flicking letter-opener. For a brief second the music and sound start to whizz us back through time

Steven (*dreamily*) I beg your pardon, sir?

The music and sound stop as Mr Pilsworth stops waggling the letter-opener and turns to Jeff

Mr Pilsworth (*to Jeff*) Is he going deaf?
Jeff I'm not quite sure what his problem is, sir.
Mr Pilsworth (*to Steven*) I said — (*starting to waggle the letter-opener again*)

During this the music and sound start up again

— you and Mr Walters will get Mrs Clarke out of her house so that it can be demolished in order for Mr Robertson to complete his shopping centre by ——
Steven (*going cross-eyed*) Do you think you could just stop wiggling — (*He holds Mr Pilsworth's hand*)

Mr Pilsworth pulls it free. The music and sound stop

Mr Pilsworth Shut up!

Miss Dixon enters from DL

Miss Dixon Sorry to interrupt, Mr Pilsworth, but Mr Robertson is getting impatient.
Mr Pilsworth Send him in.
Steven Hold it, Miss Dixon. (*To Mr Pilsworth*) Let Jeff handle this alone. It's not right for me to meet Mr Robertson when I ——

Mr Pilsworth reverts to waving his letter-opener. Music and sound start up again

Mr Pilsworth The point is Mr Robertson wants to meet you, Steven. Because I've told Mr Robertson that Mr Tancred and Mr Walters are the most reliable lawyers in Windsor. So Mr Tancred will agree with everything that Mr Walters says and simply nod his head.

During the above Steven has "gone". He turns and "walks" out of the scene

Mr Pilsworth continues to address "Steven" although Steven has now gone

Have you got that, Steven?

The Lighting and sound whizz us back through time

Mr Pilsworth (*off; echoing*) Have you got that, Steven? Have you got that? You got that...?

SCENE 4

A Chicago Nightclub. 1929

Music **No. 3b**

In the top right corner with his back to the audience is the piano player playing a honky-tonk version of "You're Gonna Love Chicago"

Johnny and Fingers appear in a spotlight UC

Johnny is nervously smoking a cigarette. Fingers is looking grim

The Lighting opens up and we are in the noisy boisterous, smoke-filled night-club. Bugs is sitting at his table DR *drinking, with two of his gangsters standing behind him. On Bugs' lap sits his "Moll", Ruby. Gangsters and gals are sitting at tables with a waiter busily serving them*

Fingers walks down to Bugs followed by the nervous Johnny

Bugs (*holding up his hand to prevent Fingers talking*) OK Ruby! Go get yourself a drink at the bar. I got business with Fingers — then I got business with my baby! Know what I mean? (*He leers at Ruby then smacks her butt and sends her off*)

Ruby stops and gives Bugs a disdainful look, then mingles with the customers

(*To Fingers*) OK! Give!

Fingers Good news, Bugs.

Bugs So give!

Fingers Two of Mr Capone's gang got early retirement.

Frankie } (*together*) { Yeah! Great!
Sammy } { You did it, Bugs!

Bugs So why'd the job take two and a half hours?

Fingers Ask the new get-away driver! (*He angrily pulls Johnny across him to Bugs*)

Johnny I'm real sorry, Mr Moran, but I'd never seen guys gunned down before! I mean the two of 'em were just gettin' a shave and Fingers blasted 'em apart. Blood was flyin' everywhere!

Bugs But why'd the job take two and a half hours, Johnny?

Johnny I threw up.

Bugs You threw up?!

Johnny On the sidewalk.

Bugs So, throwin' up don't take two and a half hours.

Johnny Well, then I got in the car. I drove the car and — er — well, I ran out of gas.

Bugs You ran out of gas?! Nothin' like that ever happened when your old man was behind the wheel!

Johnny Mr Moran, I know I goofed. I mean, the gas. Then gettin' a flat tyre —

Bugs You got a flat tyre?!

Johnny Yeah, I reckon that's why I ran into the fire hydrant —

Bugs (*furiously standing*) You ran into the f—?!

Johnny Mr Moran! Honest! I don't reckon I'm cut out to be a gangster.

Bugs That is the stupidest remark I've ever heard! Your old man was Louis May!

Johnny (*nervously*) Yeah, I know, but I kept tellin' Dad, I wanna raise chickens and live on a farm.

Everybody in the club freezes and stares at Johnny

Bugs (*grimly*) A farm?!

Fingers A farm?!

All (*except Johnny*) A farm?!

No. 4 You're Gonna Love Chicago

Johnny   I dream of a farm in the country

Fingers (*amazed*) The country?

Johnny   A homestead in old Idaho

Fingers (*puzzled*) Ida — where?
Bugs I dunno!
Johnny   With nothin' to do 'cept gaze at the view
Frankie   And worry 'bout how much you owe!
Fingers   Just look at all we got in Chicago
Sammy   And now we're gonna cut you a slice
Gangsters   You don't need a farm in the country
Bugs (*menacing*)   You just need some friendly advice
Gangsters (*in harmony*) Friendly advice
Bugs Tell him about Chicago, boys.
Fingers   There's many a sweet little racket
Sammy   That'll make you a neat little packet
Frankie   Just hurry on down to the wrong side of
                        town
Gangsters (*patting their jackets*)   With a neat little piece in your
                        jacket
Frankie   'Cos Johnny the action is hot here
Sammy   Just think of the folks who got shot
                        here
Fingers   Now don't be afraid
                        That you won't make the grade
Bug (*pulling Johnny close*) You only just got here!
All (*except Johnny*)   You're gonna love Chicago
                        Just stop and feel the buzz
                        Runnin' through yer veins boy
                        Is what Chicago does —
Bugs Here kid, have a cigar!
Johnny I'm tryin' to quit, Mr Moran
Bugs (*ramming a cigar in Johnny's mouth*) Not any more. (*He lights
it*)

Johnny coughs

(*Singing*)   For you are Louis May's boy
                        And he was a man and a half
                        You wanna quit Chicago?
                        Huh, don't make me laugh!

Bugs Hey Fingers! Fix the kid up with a shooter.
Fingers Here kid. (*He hands Johnny a gun*)
Johnny (*nervous*) Wh — what da — da do I do with this?
Fingers Just tell 'em to stick 'em up!
Johnny (*very nervous*) Er st—st—st—st—stick 'em up! (*He closes his
eyes and raises his gun*)

Everybody in the room ducks. He fires accidentally and shatters a glass held by one of the customers. The customer looks at the glass and faints

Bugs What did I tell you? The kid's a natural.
Johnny But Mr Moran, you don't understand —
Bugs So tell me.
Johnny (*singing*)   It ain't that I'm truly unwillin'
                           To make with the shootin' 'n' killin'
                           But deep in my heart, there's a kind of a part
                           That don't find the killin' too thrillin'
                           You know I ain't got much ambition
                           Except to go huntin' an' fishin'
                           I dream o' that farm with a girl on my arm —
Bugs   — You can't spend a lifetime wishin'
All (*except Johnny*) You're gonna love Chicago!
                           In spite of what you think
                           'Cos things 'll soon look diff'rent

Bugs Just get this boy a drink
Johnny No thanks, I don't — er — drink.
Bugs (*gesturing to the waiter*) Make that a double!

Johnny knocks back a double, and shudders from the effect

         (*Singing*)   You'll learn to love this city
                            And kiss that farm goodbye!
                            Chicago ain't for you kid?
                            Boo hoo — don't make me cry!
         (*Snapping his fingers*) Hey Ruby! Over here! Come to Poppa!

A disinterested Ruby appears

         (*Pulling her to him*) This is Johnny May.
Ruby (*flatly*) Hi, Johnny May.
Johnny (*politely*) Nice to meet you, Miss Ruby.
Ruby (*to Bugs*) Where'd you find him?
Bugs He's the new boy. His dad was the greatest.
Ruby Oh, yeah!
Bugs (*laughing*) Only Johnny wants to raise chickens and live on a farm in Idy-widy-ho!

The gangsters laugh

He's got a lot to learn. You tell him, Ruby doll. (*He pushes Ruby towards Johnny. Ruby mixes with the molls and the gangsters*)

Ruby (*singing*) Well honey this city is brimmin'
With plenty of good lookin' wimmin
We'll get you a suit and a floozy to boot
And plenty of hooch you can swim in
You're gonna grow fond of the city
Where even the gangsters are pretty
You'll find that ole' farm will be losin' its charm
And soon you'll be singin' this ditty
All (*except Johnny*) You're gonna love Chicago
You'll never get away!
You're gonna love this city
For ever and a day!

Two of the floozies approach Johnny. 1st Floozy puts her arm around his neck

1st Floozy (*loosening Johnny's tie*) Just try and relax.
Johnny I — I — I — I — I am relaxed.
2nd Floozy (*kneeling and squeezing his thigh*) Try harder.

All girls (*singing*) You'd love this town already
If kid you weren't so wet
Chicago ain't for you kid?
You ain't seen nothin' yet!

Ruby and the girls go into an eye-poppingly sexy vigorous dance number. Johnny is transfixed. The girls are now joined by everybody

All (*except Johnny*) You're gonna love Chicago!
Don't mind that other stuff
For once you love Chicago
You'll never get enough
For there's no other city
Can make your dream come true
You're gonna love Chicago!!
And Chicago — Chicago will love —
You —oo-oo-oo-oo-oo-oo!
Chicago loves you
An' you, too!

End of number

Bugs (*laughing and grabbing Johnny's face in his hands*) I'll look after you, kid. That was a promise I gave your dad before he died. Now get out of here!

He breaks away and grabs Ruby who is talking to one of the other girls

Get your coat, baby. I feel like an early night. Know what I mean?! (*He smacks her butt and propels her off*)

Ruby stops and looks at Bugs disdainfully, before hurrying off

Johnny has been watching this, feeling awkward

During the ensuing dialogue a gangster enters the club, gives Bugs a piece of paper and exits

Bugs reads it

Johnny Mr Moran — don't think I ain't grateful — and I know the promise you gave Dad — but what I was sayin' about the farm and the chickens ——
Bugs Hold it kid! Hold it! (*Reading for a moment longer then bursts into laughter*) Hey, you guys! Fingers!

Fingers and the two gangsters join Bugs

It did the trick, boys. We bump off two of his hoods — hey presto — Al has finally decided he wants to meet up and talk business.

The gangsters cheer wildly

OK! Let's go meet Mr Capone!

During the above a doleful Ruby has entered wearing a coat. She carries a BRIGHT Red Purse

Johnny (*standing up*) Shall I get my car, Mr Moran?
Bugs No. We'll use Fingers' car. This is one time I gotta make sure we get there.

The gangsters laugh

Shuttup! (*To Ruby*) Oh, yeah. Ruby! Change of plans, doll. (*Grinning*)

I gotta "little business" to attend to with Mr Capone. You keep it hot
for Poppa, yeah? (*He pulls her in*)

The gangsters laugh. Ruby doesn't

Johnny! You look after the lady, OK? Fingers! Boys! This is it!

Bugs leaves followed by the other gangsters, all talking excitedly

Fingers   I knew you'd do it, Bugs!
1st Gangster (*together; as they go*)   You're the big cheese, Bugs!
                                             You're the king!
2nd Gangster   You show Mr Capone who's
                                             the boss, Bugs!

Bugs (*off; interrupting*) Shut up!

*There is an awkward silence between Johnny and Ruby. She sits and
pours herself a drink*

Johnny (*finally*) Shall I sit down?
Ruby That's why they provide chairs.
Johnny Hey, that's funny, Miss Ruby. "Provide chairs".

*Ruby gives him a "Where do you come from" look. He sits and smiles at
Ruby who surveys him*

Ruby (*filling her glass and looking at Johnny*) You drinkin'?
Johnny No thanks, Miss Ruby, I don't.
Ruby Smoke?
Johnny No, I don't. Well, I do but I'm tryin' to kick it. I'm down to one
pack a day.
Ruby Why do you wanna kick it for God's sake?
Johnny Well, that's what killed Dad off. I just thought I owed it to him.
You know, to try to stop. He was in a real bad way before he died.
Pains in his chest. Coughin' all night. Couldn't get his breath when he
walked up ——
Ruby (*interrupting*) OK! I don't need a Coroner's report! So! You
don't drink. You don't smoke. What the hell do you do?
Johnny I drive the car for Mr Moran.
Ruby (*giving him a world weary look*) This is gonna be one hell of a
night! (*She downs her drink and looks at Johnny for a moment then
stands up*)

Johnny, at a loss, smiles and stands up

You wanna go for a drive?
Johnny (*blankly*) A drive?
Ruby In a "motor car".
Johnny (*hastily sitting*) Oh, no, I couldn't do nothin' like that.
Ruby Hey, I'm suggestin' a drive not a roll in the hay.
Johnny No, of course not! But — er —you know, if Mr Moran comes back and you're not here —
Ruby The meeting with Capone will go on all night. This is the big one. Dividing up the territory. Come on. Let's get some air. (*She pulls him up*)
Johnny (*sitting*) No, I don't — er — I mean, if Mr Moran finds out, he'll kick your teeth in. He'll probably blow my brains out!
Ruby You're OK, you're my "chaperone". You're Louis May's son, for crissake! (*She pulls him up*)
Johnny (*quickly sitting*) No, thanks. Some other — er —
Ruby Come on. (*She pulls him up*)
Johnny It's real nice of you, Miss Ruby, but no, I — er (*sitting*) I — er — (*looking into her eyes*) I — er — (*standing*) OK, let's go!

They hurry out

Music **No. 4a**

Mr Pilsworth (*off; echoing*) Have you got that, Steven? Have you got that — got that — got that — ?

<h2 style="text-align:center">Scene 5</h2>

Overlooking The Lake. 1929

It is night time. The "Backdrop" is the twinkling lights of Chicago in the distance. Johnny and Ruby are sitting on a bench

Ruby Have you got that kid? Listen to what I'm tellin' you. You don't just walk away from the Moran gang, you poor sap.
Johnny Mr Moran will understand though, won't he? I mean, he'll listen?
Ruby Yeah, sure Bugs'll listen. Then he'll put your feet in a pair of cement shoes and dump you in the river.
Johnny (*earnestly*) But I gotta get out of Chicago, Ruby. This ain't the life for me.

Ruby It ain't the life for me neither, but Johnny, there's no way out.
Johnny (*astonished*) Why would you want out? You're Bugs' girl.
Ruby I'm Bugs' "broad". Do you know where that puts me on a scale
of one to ten?
Johnny Ten, I guess.
Ruby Zero.
Johnny But you're Bugs Moran's broad. You're somebody!
Ruby Where have you been hidin', Johnny May? This is nineteen
twenty-nine, kid. There's no work. Some people got no food. Some of
us got no dignity — so we do what we have to do.

There is a slightly awkward pause

(*Looking at him for a moment; smiling*) You got a broad, Johnny
May?
Johnny (*with bravado*) I got more broads than I can deal with.
Ruby (*grinning*) Wow! How many? (*She leans forward and looks at
him*)
Johnny Well, let's see now. Er —
Ruby On a scale of one to ten, say.
Johnny Oh, about — er — (*capitulating*) zero.
Ruby (*smiling*) You got somethin' to look forward to then. (*She gives
him a "peck" on the cheek*)

A prolonged "music punctuation" is heard

*They both look amazed and turn to each other — then quickly turn
away and look upstage at the skyline of Chicago*

No. 5 One Of Those Moments

Ruby (*turning to the audience*; *with apprehension*)   I guess this is one
of those moments
Where the Jane kinda falls for the Joe
Tho' she knows this is one of those moments
She oughta say "whoa!"
An' yet this is one of those evenin's
With a sprinklin' of stars in the sky
When all that is missin'
From moments like this
Is the girl gettin' kissed by the guy
(*She turns upstage*)

Johnny (*turning to the audience; with apprehension*) I guess this is one
                        of those moments
                        Where the Joe an' the Jane get entwined
                        Tho' he knows he should put all these
                            feelin's
                        Right out of his mind
                        An' yet this is one of those love songs
                        That make all the others seem tame
                        There ain't no dismissin'
                        A moment like this
                        When the guy feels like kissin' the dame.

Both   Maybe I oughta act stupid
                        An' make like it don't mean a lot
                        But try as I might to stop cupid
                        His arrows are hittin' the spot
                        I guess this is one of those moments
                        Where the Jane an' the Joe get intense
                        Tho' they know it's the sort of a moment
                        That doesn't make sense
                        The night an' the stars an' the moonlight
                        We just can't keep our feet on the ground
                        There ain't no discussin'
                        It ain't right for us
                        There's no point in fussin' around ...

During the above they have moved away from each other

Break in song. Music continues

*During this they lovingly edge towards each other. Johnny goes to kiss
Ruby*

Ruby Johnny, this is madness!
Johnny If this is madness, let's check into the asylum! (*He goes to
    grab her*)
Ruby (*stopping him*) Johnny! Bugs'll blow us apart.
Johnny But I ain't never felt nothin' like that before.
Ruby (*stepping back*) Johnny!
Johnny Didn't you get the same feelin'?
Ruby (*stepping back*) Johnny!
Johnny Did you Ruby?!
Ruby (*succumbing*) Oh, boy, did I get that feelin'! (*She runs to him*)

They grab each other's hands

Johnny (*singing*)	I guess this is one of those moments
Ruby	Ooh… one of those moments
Johnny	That the guy an' the gal can't resist
Ruby	Can't resist
Johnny	Yeah this truly is one of those moments
Ruby	One of those moments
Both	That shouldn't be missed
	With the Joe an' the Jane an' the moonlight
	All the usual conditions apply
	There ain't much amiss with an evenin' like this
	With the hours creepin' blissfully by.

They are still separated but start leaning in to each other to kiss

	An' a girl with that look in her eye
Johnny	Oh my
Both	Who just oughta get kissed by the guy …

Number ends

Johnny and Ruby still haven't kissed

The following verse is accompanied only by a high string note

Johnny sings as he moves away from Ruby who is desperately waiting to be embraced

Johnny	I guess this is one of those moments
	Where the guy has his head in a whirl
	An' ends up confessin'

He can resist no longer and starts to walk back towards Ruby

He longs to progress
To gently caressin' the —

During the above last two lines the lighting changes and the singing segues into an echoey sound as he holds out his hands to Ruby —

SCENE 6

Mr Pilsworth's Office. Present Day

Mr Pilsworth, Jeff and Miss Dixon "walk" back into their original positions. As "Johnny" goes to kiss Ruby, Ruby walks out of the scene as Miss Dixon replaces her. Steven takes Miss Dixon's hands and kisses her. Her eyes are wide open in amazement. Mr Pilsworth, astonished, looks at Jeff who is frozen to the spot. Steven gathers Miss Dixon in his arms and the kiss becomes passionate. Miss Dixon finally eases herself out of the embrace and staggers back. Once more Mr Pilsworth looks back to the bewildered Jeff

Mr Pilsworth (*to Steven; in disbelief*) What the hell do you think you're doing?
Steven (*happily*) What?

Mr Pilsworth, agog, once again, looks to Jeff who has gone totally blank. Pause

Jeff (*brightly*) Happy birthday, Miss Dixon! (*He moves to her and kisses her passionately then releases her and smiles all around*)
Miss Dixon (*blankly*) It's not my birthday, Mr Walters.
Jeff (*with mock surprise*) What? Sorry, Steve. I gave you the wrong date. (*To Miss Dixon*) Have another one for good luck. (*He kisses her again*)
Miss Dixon (*bemused*) Mr — er — Robertson is — er — Mr Robertson is —er — Mr Robertson — er — says he's getting impatient.
Mr Pilsworth (*throwing the letter-opener onto his desk*) I'll go and bring him in. (*To Steven*) Remember, nod your head and agree with everything Jeff says — and for God's sake try to look intelligent.

He hurries out. Miss Dixon hesitates, looks at Steven and Jeff, then hurries out after MrPilsworth

Jeff (*turning on Steven*) What the hell was all that about?!
Steven Oh, my God, Jeff, it was so real!
Jeff No. Suddenly kissing Miss Dixon like that was unreal.
Steven I thought I was kissing Ruby.
Jeff Who the hell's Ruby?
Steven She's Bugs Moran's broad and Johnny May's fallen for her, but we've got to get away from the mob. What the hell am I going to do?
Jeff Take a very strong sedative.

Steven Everything was fine until that wretched Dr Patel started waving his thing in front of my eyes.
Jeff Hold it. Get a grip on yourself. There's no Bugs Moran. There's no Johnny May. No Ruby. And you don't need Ruby 'cos you've got a very sexy fiancée along the corridor. And if you don't fancy your sexy fiancée any more, I'll be more than happy to take over!
Steven (*suddenly*) Jeff, how long was I under? You know, regressed?
Jeff I didn't even know you were "regressed". Pilsworth was in the middle of telling us about Mr Robertson, when you suddenly grabbed Miss Dixon and gave her one hell of a smacker.
Steven As quick as that? I was in nineteen twenty-nine for hours. (*Suddenly seeing the letter-opener*) Pilsworth's letter-opener! (*He picks up the letter-opener*)
Jeff What?
Steven This is what sent me back. It had the same effect as Dr Patel's pendant.
Jeff Never mind pendants and letter-openers, we've got to sort out Mrs Emily Beatrice Clarke.
Steven I tell you, Ruby is gorgeous! I mean, although she's Mr Moran's broad she's really very sweet. You know, vulnerable.

Jeff is looking at Steven agog

I think she and Johnny might — (*He suddenly grins foolishly*) She's really sexy, Jeff.
Jeff Wait a minute! Whoa, whoa, whoa!!
Steven Hey! I wonder what happened after that kiss?
Jeff Steven!
Steven I'm not waiting a whole week to find out! (*He madly waggles the letter-opener in front of his eyes*)
Jeff (*grabbing the letter-opener*) Give me that!
Steven (*grabbing it back*) It's OK. I'll be back in a couple of seconds. (*He madly starts waggling again*) Nineteen twenty-nine! Come and get me!
Jeff Stop that! (*He grabs him and attempts to take the letter-opener*)
Steven I think Johnny's fallen for her! Come and get me, Ruby!

In the ensuing struggle Steven lays back on the desk. Jeff leans over him

Mr Pilsworth enters followed by Miss Dixon carrying a tray of coffee

They stop in astonishment on seeing the struggling pair, with Jeff laying across Steven

Jeff Give it to me!
Steven This could be love, Jeff. Real love! Come and get me!
Jeff Give it to me now!

By now Mr Pilsworth is staring in disbelief

Steven Where are you?! I'm waiting for you! I want you!
Mr Pilsworth (*outraged*) Gentlemen!

Steven and Jeff stop their struggle and disentangle themselves

Mr Pilsworth (*turning to the open-mouthed Miss Dixon*) Put it down,
girl, and get out.

In a daze Miss Dixon gives the tray to Mr Pilsworth

Get out!

Miss Dixon scuttles out

Are you two "on something", for God's sake?! (*Turning and calling*)
This way, Mr Robertson.

*Mr Robertson enters and Steven's mouth opens in disbelief — Mr
Robertson is an exact image of Bugs Moran. (Not surprising as they
are played by the same actor) Mr Robertson is a Cockney millionaire*

Mr Robertson I'm a busy man Pilsworth. Let's cut to the chase.
Mr Pilsworth Of course. May I present Mr Walters.
Jeff Very pleased to meet you, sir.
Mr Robertson Jeff.

They shake hands

(*To Steven*) And you must be Mr Tancred.

*Steven is standing there, dumbstruck. Mr Robertson shakes Steven's
hand vigorously. Steven drops Mr Robertson's hand*

Steven (*backing away, horrified; pointing*) Bugs! Bugs!! Bugs!!!

*Music **No. 5a***

*Mr Robertson looks bewildered and turns to Jeff. Jeff is momentarily
fazed*

Jeff Good thinking, Steve! "Bugs"! Excuse me, Mr Robertson, we have
to check for bugs. (*Quickly lifting a surprised Mr Robertson's arms in
the air, separating his legs and frisking him*) No, he's clean. No bugs.
It's office policy, Mr Robertson. Can't be too careful these days can
we, Mr Pilsworth?

*He separates an outraged Mr Pilsworth's legs, but stops as Mr Pilsworth
hastily protects himself*

Right. All safe and sound. Over to you, Mr Robertson. (*He smiles
politely at Mr Robertson who looks totally bemused*)

Music **No. 5b**

SCENE 7

By The River in Windsor. Two Weeks Later. Present Day

*Steven and Barbara are sitting on a bench by the river. Barbara is on
her mobile and eating a sandwich. Steven is lost in thought, smoking a
cigarette and feeding the ducks*

Barbara (*on mobile*) Mrs Truscott! We are going for fifty percent of
your husband's assets, plus maintenance, plus support for the children,
plus upkeep for the household pets! Well, get some!... (*Ringing off*)
Women!

Steven is lost in his own world

I don't even have to ask what you're thinking about.
Steven I just can't get Johnny and Ruby out of my head.
Barbara Steven, for the last two weeks you have been the star of the
office emails! Kissing Miss Dixon in front of Daddy. Yelling for this
Ruby to come and take you back to nineteen twenty-nine. Calling Mr
Robertson "Bugs"!
Steven He is Bugs!
Barbara No he's not! He's our meal ticket for the next six months.
You've got to pull yourself together!
Steven Look, all this must be happening to me for a reason. God knows
what but I don't understand why you won't even discuss it with me.
(*Taking her hand*) Come and see Dr Patel with me.
Barbara I've told you, no more Dr Patel!
Steven All right, all right! I cancelled, I cancelled! (*Pause; He returns
to feeding the ducks*)

Barbara (*gently*) Steven, please! Will you forget Johnny — and forget Ruby.

He looks at her expressionless

(*Rising to go, hesitating then taking the cigarette from him and stubbing it out*) And don't forget we're seeing the caterers at five thirty!
Steven Caterers?
Barbara For our wedding! We're getting married, remember!
Steven (*smiling*) It's in my Blackberry.
Barbara (*managing a smile*) It's a good job I love you.
Steven Me you, too
Barbara (*suddenly serious*) It's kind of weird, though, me having a rival in nineteen twenty-nine.
Steven (*looking surprised*) Ruby's Johnny's girl.
Barbara (*simply*) You are Johnny, aren't you?

They look at each other for a moment

I'm due in court at two.
Steven Good luck.
Barbara (*moving, stopping and turning; gently*) What's Ruby got that I haven't?

Barbara goes

Steven stays looking after her for a moment. He then turns back, pensively

No. 6 The Thing About Ruby

Steven   The thing about Ruby
              She's diff'rent not better
              Just diff'rent there is no right or wrong
              The thing about Barbara
              You'd write her a letter
              With Ruby you'd write her a song
              The truth about Barbara
              It's simple, I love her
              So simple — she's ev'rything to me
              The truth about Ruby
              She made me discover

I'm not in the place I should be.

I'm caught in the present
But lost in the past
Yet time still continues to flow
The thing about Ruby
Is how could it last
When our future has nowhere to go?

The thing about Barbara
You'd write her a letter
With Ruby you'd write her a song.

Steven turns and walks into Dr Patel's consulting room

Barbara (*echoing voice over*) And no more Dr Patel! No more Dr Patel...!

SCENE 8

Dr Patel's Consulting Room. Present Day

Dr Patel enters immediately

Dr Patel (*shaking Steven's hand*) Good to see you again, Steven! When you cancelled all your appointments I thought you had given up on me. (*He indicates for Steven to lie on the couch*)
Steven (*doing so*) Yes, I'm sorry. I'm under a bit of pressure at the moment.
Dr Patel So, how about your smoking? Any improvement?
Steven Definitely. I'm up to forty a day.
Dr Patel (*smiling*) So let's see what we can do about this nicotine addiction.
Steven This is more like Ruby addiction.
DrPatel Now, Steven — relax. Clear your mind. (*He starts to swing the pendant*)

Music **No. 6a**

Deep breaths. Watch the pendant. Listen to my voice. Calm — all is calm. Calm.
Steven (*happily*) Yes! Yes! Johnny and Ruby! They're together. I'm so happy for them! (*He stands up and walks* SR)

Ruby enters from DR

Dr Patel continues to look at where Steven was on the couch

SCENE 9

Johnny's small Chicago apartment. 1929

The set appears DR. *There is a door to the bedroom* DR *and a door from the apartment into the corridor upstage. The only furniture is a small table and a chair. Ruby's Red Purse is on the chair*

Steven (*off; echoing*) I'm so happy for them!
Dr Patel (*off; echoing*) Relax, Steven, calm.

Steven becomes Johnny in a passionate embrace with Ruby. Ruby is wearing a flimsy dressing gown

Steven (*off; echoing*) It's real love — love — love.
Johnny (*breaking the embrace; emotionally torn*) I hate you, Ruby!
Ruby (*putting her hand to Johnny's lips*) Johnny!
Johnny I don't hate you, I love you, Ruby, but it's drivin' me crazy!
Ruby We got something great goin' here, baby.
Johnny No, it ain't great! I can't go on livin' like this. Havin' to watch Bugs treat you the way he does.
Ruby I can deal with it! (*She picks up her Red Purse and takes out a packet of cigarettes*)
Johnny I can't! You havin' to go back to Bugs' bed every night!
Ruby Johnny! (*She breaks away and throws her Red Purse onto the table*)
Johnny (*pressing on*) I love you, Ruby, and it's killin' me! (*He pulls her to him*)
Ruby I love you too, Johnny — but there ain't no way out of this!
Johnny Yes there is. We gotta kick this town. The both of us. I'm tellin' Bugs today. I'm quittin' the gang!

There is a sudden knocking on the door. Fearful, they break and look to the door

Fingers (*off*) Hey! Johnny! It's me, Fingers!

Johnny and Ruby look at one another

Johnny (*whispering*) In the bedroom. (*He quickly and silently ushers Ruby into the bedroom*)

Ruby exits holding the cigarette packet

Johnny shuts the bedroom door

Fingers (*off*) Hey! Open the door!
Johnny OK, Fingers! I'm comin'! I'm comin'! (*Opening the door; cheerfully*) Hi, Fingers!

Johnny lets Fingers in

Fingers OK, kid, let's go.
Johnny (*trying to be nonchalant*) What d'you mean, "let's go"?
Fingers Bugs wants to see you. At the garage.
Johnny OK, OK You — er — you go on. I'll be with you in a coupla minutes.
Fingers He wants to see you now. There's a meetin'. Urgent! The whole gang. The North Street garage!
Johnny Yeah, but, Fingers —
Fingers No "buts" kid!
Johnny But I gotta —
Fingers (*pressing on*) You gotta come with me now. Get out!

Fingers pushes Johnny out and starts to follow — but stops

Dark music **No. 6b** *creeps in*

Fingers has seen Ruby's Red Purse on the table. He hesitates then picks it up and slowly looks to the closed bedroom door

Expressionless, he puts the purse in his overcoat pocket and leaves

The dark music continues and the Lights take us through to the next scene

SCENE 10

Interior of the North Street Garage and the Street. 1929

The Lighting favours the downstage street area with the interior of the garage in eerie shadow upstage. The interior takes up about three quarter of the upstage area with the rear wall starting UR. *A small section of the side wall, in which is a metal door, comes down from* ULC *— the wall then continues in an imaginary line* DS. *The metal door leads into an alley which runs from* UL *to* DL. *There is a large window in the rear wall under which is a pile of old tyres. A door in the right wall leads to the storeroom*

In frozen silhouette Bugs and the gang are in a group, waiting. They carry their guns. The Young Bum sits on the corner of the street, DL

Fingers enters the street from DR *followed by Johnny*

Johnny Hey, Fingers! Hold it. What's this meetin' all about? Why all the secrecy for Crissake?

Fingers ignores him and walks upstage towards the garage door

(*Approaching the Young Bum taking out his wallet*) Here take this, kid. Get yourself a coffee and a bagel. (*He hands the Young Bum a dollar bill*)
The Young Bum Gee, thanks, Johnny. This'll buy dinner for Ma and the whole family.

The Young Bum hurries off

Fingers (*banging loudly on the garage door*) Open up, it's Fingers and Johnny! (*He grabs Johnny*)

The Lighting comes up on the interior as the first Gangster opens the door

Get in there! (*He pushes Johnny in*)
Bugs (*stepping forward*) What kept you, Johnny?
Johnny Sorry, Mr Moran.
Bugs Over there kid.

Johnny joins the rest of the gang. He then indicates for the first Gangster

and Fingers to join the others. They do

OK! Now — do you want the good news or the bad news?
Gangsters (*together*) ⎧ Good.
⎩ Bad.
⎨ Give us the good.
⎩ Let's have the bad.
Bugs Shut up! I'll give you the good — Capone has offered to split Chicago right down the middle. Fifty-fifty. Half Al Capone, half Bugs Moran.

The Gangsters cheer and shout and raise their tommy-guns

Gangsters (*together*) ⎧ You did it, Bugsy!
⎨ Great!
⎪ You showed him, Bugs.
⎩ Terrific!
Bugs Shut up! Now, the bad news — Bugs Moran ain't accepting Mr. Capone's offer.

There is a murmur of surprise

Because — and this is the *best* news — Bugs Moran is gonna have one hundred percent of Chicago!

There is a brief pause and then whoops of delight and cheers as the gang raise their tommy-guns

No. 7 Rat-a-Tat Rag

Bugs

Brush your hat "n" polish your shoes
We're gonna have some fun
Rat-Tat-Tat who's makin' the news?
It's good old tommy-gun
We're gonna govern the zone now
— Dat is my personal brag!
Maybe you'll even see Al Capone now
Dancin' the Rat-a-Tat Rag

Bugs and Gangsters

Pitter Pat start tappin' those feet
It's music time again
Rat-Tat-Tat who's takin' the heat?
It's Bugs' merry men

> We gonna make a big noise now
> We got this town in the bag
> You'll see Capone and his dancin' boys now
> Doin' the Rat-a-Tat Rag

Fingers Just one tiny point Bugs. How exactly you gonna get one hundred percent of Chicago.

Bugs I'll tell ya. We got this fifty-fifty offer from Al because we bumped off two of his gang, right?

Gangsters Yeah!

Fingers That's right boss!

Bugs So how do we get ourselves a hundred percent?

The Gangsters have no answer

> OK. I'll tell ya! We knock off the rest of the gang — and Capone himself!

All Wow!

Bugs (*singing*)	Al an' his gang are goin' to perdition
Fingers	Just hope we have enough ammunition
Both	Then we'll assume the top dog position
Gangsters	We're the hoods who'll handle the goods — yeah!
Both	It's just a minor assassination Then we'll control the whole situation
Fingers	Bugs an' his gang'll get an ovation
Bugs	We'll go down an' conquer the town — yeah!

Fingers Great plan, Bugs. Just one thing. How you gonna get Capone to co-operate?

All Yeah, yeah!

Bugs Shut up! Al and his top boys are coming here tonight.

Gangsters Tonight?

Bugs Yeah, why wait? Al thinks the meeting is to agree to the two territories. Instead of which — when they come through that door — (*Miming shooting a tommy-gun*) Ha ha ha ha ha ha ha!

Bugs and Gangsters (*singing*) Dear old Al is gonna get slugged
> An' what a big surprise!
> Listen pal he's gonna get plugged
> An' right between the eyes!

> We're gonna conquer Chicago
> Soon they will need a white flag
> You'll see Capone an' his whole farrago
> Doin' the Rat-a-Tat Rag!

Bugs picks up a tommy-gun, grins and mimes shooting

16 bar tap break

> We're about to quicken the pace
> So grab your violin
> Empty out that black leather case
> An' put your shooter in
> You'll see Capone lookin' swell there
> Down at the morgue with a tag
> All of his gang'll be down in hell, yeah
> Doin' the Rat-a-Tat

Bugs   You dirty Rat-a-Tat
Bugs and Gangsters   Doin' the Rat-a-Tat Rag!

Number ends

Bugs OK. Over here kid.

Johnny steps to Bugs

Tonight, Johnny. You become a man. (*He kisses Johnny on both cheeks*)
Johnny (*lightly*) I thought I was a man already, Mr Moran.
Bugs No, Johnny. As of now you're being promoted to hit man! (*He thrusts his tommy-gun into Johnny's arms*)
Johnny (*looking at it, his thoughts racing; blankly*) Hit man?
Bugs OK, Johnny. Be here at six o'clock tonight when you help wipe out Capone and his gang.

The Gangsters, whooping and yelling, grab the confused Johnny and rush him out

(*Yelling after them*) Shut up!
Fingers Bugs — I think there's something you ought to know.
Bugs (*chuckling*) What's that?

Fingers produces Ruby's purse

(*Taking it; still chuckling*) Ruby's purse. So what?
Fingers It was in Johnny's apartment.
Bugs (*still chuckling*) Yeah, so what? (*His' smile fades as he realizes the implication. He looks at the purse — his eyes narrow. He then thrusts the purse back onto Fingers and grabs him. He whispers viciously into Fingers' ear*)
Fingers (*nodding and smiling*) I like that idea, Bugs.

Music **No. 7a**

I like it.

He turns and goes

(*Off; echoing*) I like it — I like it — I like it —

Lighting and music take us through to next scene

SCENE 11

Dr Patel's Consulting Room. Present Day

Steven is on the couch. Dr Patel is standing beside him. Steven's jacket is on the back of the chair

Steven (*as Johnny; scared*) I don't like it! I don't like it! No! I don't like it!
Dr Patel All right then. Come back. You're perfectly safe.
Steven (*as Johnny*) I don't wanna be a hit man!
Dr Patel Yes, I can understand that, Steven. Come on, now. You're here. All is safe. All is calm. Back! (*He snaps his fingers*)
Steven (*looking around for a moment then looking back to Dr Patel*) I was in Chicago again.
DrPatel (*smiling*) With Ruby I gather.
Steven But it's not good. Bugs wants Johnny to be a hit man — wipe out the Capone gang.
Dr Patel And Johnny doesn't want to do that, does he?
Steven (*rising*) No! I was planning to kick Chicago. Take Ruby with me — but now — If I don't carry out Mr Moran's orders — (*Suddenly*) Put me under again! (*He sits back on the couch*)
Dr Patel I'm sorry Steven, you are in no fit state!
Steven Please!
Dr Patel Take time to assimilate what you are learning from Johnny

and discover how it relates to this life.
Steven I don't care about this life! I need to know what happened to
Johnny and Ruby!
Dr Patel (*moving to the door*) I'll see you next week.
Steven (*rising*) That might be too late!

*Jeff bursts in followed by a female receptionist who is trying to
restrain him*

Jeff (*entering*) And I tell you Mr Tancred is leaving! (*To Steven*) Right!
Come on! (*He grabs Steven and then Steven's jacket*)
Receptionist I tried to stop him, Dr Patel.
Dr Patel (*to Jeff; angrily*) What's the meaning of this, sir?
Jeff (*to Steven*) Barbara told you not to see this quack any more.
Steven I had to.
Receptionist (*to Dr Patel*) Doctor, shall I telephone the police?
Dr Patel No. (*To Jeff*) Who are you, sir?
Jeff (*to Steven*) Barbara's absolutely livid.
Steven Jeff, it's not good in nineteen twenty-nine!
Jeff It's not exactly great today! You're half an hour late for the
caterers!

Jeff pushes Steven out

(*To Dr Patel*) And you're very likely going to be sued for undue
influence on an idiot!

Jeff exits

Dr Patel (*to the receptionist*) I think that young man is in need of anger
therapy.

Music **No. 7b**

SCENE 12

Caterer's Showroom. Present Day

The large showroom is extremely elegant with the main arched entrance
UC. *The Manager of the establishment, full of charm, bonhomie, and
extravagant gestures, is with Barbara,* UC. L *is a large table with
examples of the wedding feast including a six-tiered wedding cake. There
are three other "happy couples" impatiently waiting to be attended to*

R *are three open champagne bottles in ice buckets on the table. Mrs Pilsworth is sipping from her glass. She is "merry" — but not overly so! Barbara is pacing up and down anxiously looking at her watch*

Manager You see Miss Pilsworth, I do have other couples to attend to. And if Mr Tancred —

Barbara has already stormed UC *looking for Steven. The Manager indicates "sorry" to the "three happy couples" then hurries to Mrs Pilsworth*

(*To Mrs Pilsworth; brightly*) So Mrs Pilsworth, do we have a decision?
Mrs Pilsworth (*lowering her glass*) Mm! Very nice. Barbara, try a sip.
Barbara (*loudly*) I don't want a sip, mother. I want Steven! (*She storms* UC *looking for Steven*)

The happy couples react. Mrs Pilsworth and the Manager try to smile

Mrs Pilsworth (*happily*) He'll be here, darling. (*She takes another swig*)
Manager (*scuttling across to the happy couples*) I'm so sorry to keep you happy couples waiting but — er — (*waving in the direction of Barbara*) you know — slight — er — no worries! All will be lovey-dovey. (*Scuttling behind Mrs Pilsworth to* R; *brightly*) Decision time!
Mrs Pilworth Now this is the Moet et Chandon, yes?
Manager No, that's the Dom Perignon. (*Pointing to another bottle*) This is the Moet et Chandon.
Mrs Pilsworth I'll try the Moet then.
Manager (*politely*) You already have, Mrs Pilsworth — twice.
Mrs Pilsworth (*laughing*) Is that a fact? (*Pointing to the third bottle*) And this one is —?
Manager The Lanson.
Mrs Pilsworth And have I — ?
Barbara (*returning to her mother's* L) Yes, you have, mother. Twice!
Mrs Pilsworth (*laughing*) Really? Have you tried the Lanson, Barbara?
Barbara I don't want to try any of them, mother! How could he do this to me!
Mrs Pilsworth (*cheerfully*) Just be grateful it's not the wedding day.
Barbara I'll kill him!

The happy couples react

Mrs Pilsworth   (*to the Manager*) Do you do funerals as well? (*She laughs and sips her Dom Perignon*)

Jeff pushes Steven on from UC

Steven   No Jeff, I've got a real problem.
Jeff   (*indicating Barbara*) Yes, she's right here.
Steven   It's Johnny and Ruby.
Jeff   It's you and Barbara. (*He turns Steven to Barbara*)
Barbara   (*icily*) Visiting Chicago again? (*She turns her back on Steven*)
Manager   No wonder he's late, flying in from Chicago.
Mrs Pilsworth   Have I missed a couple of sentences?!
Jeff   Hi, Barbara.

Barbara stays with her back turned

Bye, Barbara.

Jeff hurries out

Barbara turns to confront Steven

NB.   During   the   following   number   FIANCÉ=MALE! FIANCÉE=FEMALE!

No. 8 He's Having An Affair

Barbara   So, did you have a good time with Ruby?
Mrs Pilsworth   (*confused*) A good time with Ruby?
Barbara   Haven't you heard, Mother? It's all over the office.
Mrs Pilsworth   (*awkwardly*) Barbara, maybe this isn't the time.
Barbara   (*singing)*   He's having an affair with Ruby!

Barbara grabs Steven and thrusts him into a tango pose then does a tango routine with an embarrassed Steven

Everybody reacts

Manager   (*embarrassed; covering*) Perhaps we could get back to the menu!

Barbara (*singing*)   — Having an affair with Ruby!
Manager Or maybe we could look at the venue?
Steven Darling, please! I'm on my knees I didn't mean to cause you pain
Barbara (*singing*)   — Having an affair with Ruby!
Mrs Pilsworth   I'm sure the dear boy can explain!
Barbara (*speaking; to Steven*) Can you?! Can you explain your affair with Ruby! (*To the couples*) We're getting married in three weeks time! He made a promise, "I won't go back", he said. But he can't stop seeing Ruby!!
Mrs Pilsworth   He's having an affair?
Barbara   With a hooker in Chicago!
Manager   In Chicago?
Mrs Pilsworth (*to manager*) What's a hooker?
Barbara   The beast!

Manager whispers in Mrs Pilsworth's ear

Mrs Pilsworth (*realizing*) What??!!
Barbara (*singing*)   He really doesn't care
                           If we're married —
Manager   — In Chicago?
Mrs Pilsworth   — No in Windsor!
Barbara   He's not worried in the least!
                           He's cheated me!
Mrs Pilsworth   Be still my heart!
Barbara   Maltreated me!
                           Until my heart
                           Is crumpled and creased.

Steven Barbara, please! (*Simply*) I couldn't help myself.
Barbara (*to the other fiancées*) What would you do if your fiancé was spending his afternoons with a hooker in a nightclub?! Come on! (*To 1st Fiancée*) You!

The three fiancées go into their own tango routine

1st Fiancée (*singing*)   He's having an affair?
                           I'd be heartsick
1st Fiancée } (*together*) I'd be steaming!
2nd Fiancée
All Fiancées   I would smack him! (and the hooker)
                           What a dope!
Mrs Pilsworth   It's all too much to bear

Manager Does this mean the wedding's cancelled?
Mrs Pilsworth (*to Barbara*) Oh but surely you'll forgive him?
Barbara   Not a hope!
All Fiancées   I'd menace him
                               I'd mangle him
                               I'd savage him
                               I'd strangle him
Barbara   Just give me the rope!

A fiancé steps forward

1st Fiancée (*speaking*) Hold it! If he's having an affair — (*To Barbara*)
It must mean you're not giving him what he wants!
All Fiancées Not giving him what he wants!
Barbara (*proceeding to do a very sexy tango with Steven; singing*)
                               I meet all his requirements
                               He has no need to rove
                               I keep our love life cooking
                               And not only on the stove
All Fiancées   And still he's got a hooker
                               It really is a crime!
                               And simply quite amazing
                               How he finds the time!

By now the tango has had its erotic effect on Mrs Pilsworth

Dance break

*The entire company tango in the background as Mrs Pilsworth grabs the
embarrassed Manager and leads him into a mad sexy tango. By the end
of the break, Mrs Pilsworth has the Manager in a most inappropriate
tango pose*

Barbara (*speaking*) Mother!
Manager (*singing*)   Who is this other woman?
                               I think we should be told
Mrs Pilsworth   Yes! Has some old flame resurfaced?
Barbara (*nodding*)   With the emphasis on "old"
Mrs Pilsworth   He loves an older woman?
                               He really is a swine!
                               When precisely did he meet her?
Barbara   Nineteen twenty-nine

Everybody reacts

Mrs Pilsworth   (*speaking*) Nineteen twenty-nine? My God, she's over
ninety! (*She thinks about this for a moment, then laughs*)

                (*Singing*) You are a dreadful pair!
                Oh you really got me going
                But of course I don't believe a single word!
Couples and Manager   (*joining*) He's having an affair
                With a hooker in Chicago!
                Now that's quite the daftest thing I ever
                    heard!
                In future keep your fantasies
                Securely in the bedroom please!
Steven   (*speaking*) But —
Mrs Pilsworth   (*singing*) It's simply absurd!
Steven   (*speaking*) But —
Couples   (*singing*)   The daftest we've heard!
Steven   (*speaking*) But –
Mrs Pilsworth   (*singing*) Not another word!

End of Number

        (*Speaking*) So, no problems! (*Calling to the Manager*) We'll take thirty
of the Dom Perignon.
Manager   Thirty bottles of the Perignon?
Mrs Pilsworth   Cases, dear boy, cases! And now the food!

The Manager crosses in front of Steven and leads him to the table SL.
The Manager picks up his gold-plated ladle. He is now DL *with Steven
on his right*

Manager   Ah, yes! I thought for starters some "*petits batonnets de
poisson*".
Mrs Pilsworth   Petty batons — ?
Manager   Fish fingers!
Mrs Pilsworth   (*laughing gaily*) Fish fingers! I love fish fingers. Daddy
loves fish fingers too, doesn't he, Barbara? (*Chuckling merrily at
Barbara who is still looking daggers; to the Manager*) And for the
main course?
Manager   Ah! Several choices. All to die for.
Mrs Pilsworth   Oo! Exciting!

She takes Barbara across her and places her next to Steven

The situation eases somewhat

The Manager, with flamboyant gestures, indicates the various examples on the table. As fate would have it, he flicks his ladle across Steven's face pointing from dish to dish. Steven's eyes flick from side to side watching the ladle

Manager Braised English lobster with Savoy cabbage. Guinea fowl salad with black pudding…

Music **No. 8b**

…Roast salmon salad. Crab and cheddar soufflé. Roast beef with apple and horseradish coleslaw …

By now Steven has "gone" and has walked out of the scene

(*Continuing to address Steven as though he's still there*) — Smoked eel and Haddock cakes. Parfait of chicken with toasted onion brioche — all washed down with a delicious port. Tawny or the Ruby. I suggest the best Ruby.

Black-out

(*Off, echoing*) The best Ruby. The best Ruby — Ruby — Ruby—

SCENE 13

Johnny's small Chicago apartment. 1929

Johnny (*off*) Ruby! Ruby!

The door bursts open and Johnny rushes in

Ruby!

A frightened Ruby, still wearing her flimsy dressing gown comes in from the bedroom. She is smoking and carrying the packet of cigarettes

Ruby Johnny, you OK?!
Johnny There's gonna be a hit tonight. Al Capone and his boys are

gonna be wiped out. At the garage.
Ruby Oh, my God!
Johnny Bugs has made me one of the trigger men.
Ruby (*terrified*) Johnny! Whatcha gonna do?
Johnny What d'ya think? Idaho! And you're comin' with me, Ruby!
Ruby Johnny — my life's in Chicago.
Johnny This ain't no life, Ruby! (*Producing a document*) I got the
papers. Our own farm! Well, it's more like a barn with a field.
So what do you expect for ninety-five bucks?
Ruby (*gently*) Johnny, I don't want to spend the rest of my life pickin'
potatoes in Idy-Widy-Ho.
Johnny You said you loved me.
Ruby I do, Johnny but ——
Johnny But not enough, huh?

For a moment they look at each other

I'll go pack my case.

Johnny exits into the bedroom

No. 9 Deep In My Heart

Ruby   Deep in my heart I long for di'mon's
                     Now here's a man I know will never have a cent
                     Deep in my heart I love the city
                     But this is not a place
                     He'll ever be content
                     Deep in my heart I want to show him
                     That there are things about my life.

                     I have to keep
                     And then he tells me he really loves me
                     Deep in my heart I want to weep.

                     Why should I change my life forever?
                     What if I go with him and find
                     I really hate the simple life?
                     He isn't rich — he isn't clever
                     Why should I want to be his wife?

                     Deep in my heart I'm scared of runnin'
                     Why should I go with him and tear my life apart?

I need an answer — but where to find it?
I know it's here — deep in my heart.

Deep in my heart I yearn for di'mon's
Although I know that even
Di'mon's lose their gleam
Deep in my heart I love this city
But what's the good of city life without a dream?

Deep in my heart I know it's crazy
But then I guess I always
Knew that from the start
Oh I could learn to get by without him
And dream a dream or two that isn't all about him
But what's the use?
He'd still be there deep in my heart.

Number ends

Johnny comes out of the bedroom with a small suitcase

They look at each other tenderly but sadly

Johnny (*as if saying "goodbye"*) I've done my packin' baby. (*He holds up the small suitcase*)
Ruby (*saying nothing, smiling, then opening her arms*) I travel light.
Johnny (*hesitating then emotionally hugging her; realizing*) Hey! You can't go just wearin' a night shirt!
Ruby (*laughing*) OK. I'll go get a hat. You want a cigarette before we kick Chicago?
Johnny No, I've finally quit, sweetheart. Must be love, huh?
Ruby If that's what love does for you. (*She laughs, throws the packet over her shoulder and hugs him*)
Johnny You sure about this, Ruby?
Ruby One hundred percent. Potato-pickin' Idaho here we come!
Johnny Then do you know what I'm gonna do next?
Ruby What?
Johnny I'm gonna marry you, Ruby.
Ruby (*overcome*) Johnny! Does that mean we're kinda engaged?
Johnny Guess so.
Ruby Gee! And do you know what today is?
Johnny It's terrific, I know that!
Ruby It's St. Valentine's Day.

Johnny St. Valentine? Who's he?
Ruby St. Valentine! Goddess of Love or somethin'. February fourteenth.

Johnny puts his arms around her and they look front — to the future

Johnny February fourteenth, huh? We'll remember that, sweetheart.
Ruby To our dying day, Johnny.
Johnny To our dying day, Ruby.

They embrace

Black-out

> (*Off*) Ruby — Ruby — Ruby —
> **Manager** (*off; echoing*) ...Ruby...Ruby...Ruby...

Lights and music **No. 9a** *as Johnny "walks" into the next scene*

SCENE 14

Caterer's Showroom. Present Day

Steven, looking very happy, has taken his place next to the Manager

Manager ...Ruby port to finish. Choice of main course. Fish fingers to start. (*To Steven*) What do you think of that, Mr Tancred?
Steven (*as Johnny; happily*) No! There's no more Fingers for me!
Manager Well, the menu's not set in stone.
Steven (*as Johnny*) And no Bugs!
Manager Certainly not. We're most hygienic here.
Steven (*as Johnny*) Happy Valentine's Day everybody!
All Valentine's Day?
Mrs Pilsworth (*blankly*) In the middle of September?
Barbara (*tearfully and angrily*) Steven, you're embarrassing me. (*She breaks away to* c)

Steven runs after her. The Manager moves to Mrs Pilsworth

Manager (*gaily*) Perhaps, we should discuss the liqueurs.
Steven (*as Johnny; to Barbara*) We're headin' away, baby. Idaho, here we come!
Mrs Pilsworth (*nervously*) I thought it was the South of France.

Steven (*grabbing Barbara's hand; as Johnny*) OK, let's hit the —

He stops and hesitates as he "comes to". He looks around. He then looks at Barbara again

   You're Barbara.

Barbara Steven! (*She breaks away from him, nearly in tears*)

Steven looks to Mrs Pilsworth and the Manager. There is an awkward pause

Manager (*trying to smile*) I'm Nigel.
Mrs Pilsworth (*blankly*) I'm Daphne.
Steven (*to Barbara*) I thought you were Rub — Barb —
Mrs Pilsworth Rhubarb? (*Aghast; to the Manager*) He thinks she's a vegetable.
Steven (*to Barbara*) I was in nineteen twenty-nine.
Barbara Steven!

Barbara bursts into tears and runs out

Steven (*at a loss; to the couples*) Happy St Valentine's Day! (*Calling off*) Barbara!

Steven rushes off after Barbara

Mrs Pilsworth (*to the Manager*) I think I'll try the liqueurs!
Manager I think I'll join you!

They both drink

Music **No. 9b**

<h2 style="text-align:center">SCENE 15</h2>

The Reception Area of Pilsworth and Pilsworth. Present Day

Miss Dixon is at her desk DR. *She is flipping through a pile of print-outs*

Miss Dixon (*reading; à la Brooklyn*) "Bugs Moran beats laundering rap" ... "Bugs Moran indicted for tax evasion" ...

Barbara hurries in from DL *still in her tearful state*

Oh, Miss Pilsworth, Mrs Truscott has phoned several times and I've left the messages —
Barbara I don't want to know!

Barbara exits UR *towards her office*

Miss Dixon (*to the audience*) I think it's going to be another of those days. (*Returning to reading the print-outs*; *à la Brooklyn*) "Bugs Moran linked to illicit hooch haul", "Bugs Moran found not guilty in — "

Jeff hurries in from UL

Jeff Is Miss Pilsworth back yet?
Miss Dixon In her office. Not a happy bunny.

Jeff starts to move

Oh, Mr Walters!
Jeff (*impatiently*) What? What?
Miss Dixon Mr Tancred asked me to do a Google search on Bugs Moran and John May and I've ——
Jeff Throw them in the dustbin!
Miss Dixon No, but this Mr Moran. He actually existed. A real live Chicago gangster in nineteen twenty-nine.
Jeff All the more reason to throw him in the dustbin!

Jeff hurries off UR *to see Barbara*

Miss Dixon (*to audience*) It's a madhouse! (*To the print-outs*; *in a Brooklyn accent*) It's the trash can for you, Mr Moran. (*Suddenly looking serious*; *in her normal voice*) "St Valentine's Day massacre — whole gang slaughtered — February the fourteenth". You sure got yours, Mr Moran. (*Reading again*) Oh my God! Among the bodies – John May – aged twenty-three.

Steven hurries in from DL

Steven Is Miss Pilsworth back?
Miss Dixon In her office —

Steven starts to move up

(*Rising*) Mr Tancred! I've done the Google on Mr Moran for you and
I found something which ——
Steven (*interrupting*) I don't need to know anything more about
nineteen twenty-nine. I'm fine now.
Miss Dixon Well, that's good news. We've all been a bit worried about
you in the office, you know. (*Indicating "madness"*) But I think maybe
you ought to glance through this lot. (*She offers him the print-outs*)
Steven Put them on my desk. I'll save it for bedtime reading on the
honeymoon.

Steven hurries out UR

Miss Dixon (*to audience*) I'm not sure that's such a good idea.

A distraught Mrs Pilsworth enters from DL

Mrs Pilsworth Is my daughter back yet?
Miss Dixon In her office, Mrs Pilsworth.

Mrs Pilsworth goes to move

I think she might be little bit involved at the moment.
Mrs Pilsworth She needs her Mummy.

As she moves to go, a distressed Barbara hurries in from UR *followed
by Jeff and Steven*

Barbara I don't want to discuss it, Steven!
Steven Just listen, will you?!
Jeff Yes, just listen, Barbara.
Mrs Pilsworth Just listen to him, Barbara.
Steven I can handle this, Jeff!
Mrs Pilsworth Listen to him, Barbara!
Barbara I can handle this, Mother
Miss Dixon (*tentatively*) Shall I take a coffee break?
Steven (*grabbing Barbara's hands*) Barbara! I don't have to go back
any more!
Barbara You said that before!
Steven Johnny and Ruby are all right now. Their future's OK. And so
is ours. I promise you!
Barbara You've said that before, too.
Miss Dixon (*tentatively*) Shall I take a coffee break?
Mrs Pilsworth Just listen to the boy!

Barbara Mother!
Jeff Listen Barbara!
Steven I can handle this. (*To Barbara*) Please believe me! OK I've said
    that before, too.
Barbara Over and over! (*She furiously removes her engagement ring,
    thrusts it into Steven's hands and falls, weeping onto Jeff's shoulder*)

*There is a brief awkward pause. Jeff smiles. There is another slight
pause*

Miss Dixon I think I'll take a coffee break.

Miss Dixon exits DR *as an angry Mr Pilsworth enters from* UR

Mr Pilsworth What was all that shouting about?!
Mrs Pilsworth (*tearfully*) Barbara's broken off the engagement,
    Gregory.
Mr Pilsworth What?!
Steven This is all my fault, Mr Pilsworth.
Mr Pilsworth (*furiously*) So what's different?!
Steven Me! I'm different as of today! (*He grabs Barbara's hands in
    his*)

No. 10 The Best is Yet to Come

(*to Barbara; singing*)   I hardly knew
                          How much I needed you
                          Until I nearly threw it all away
                          But then I saw
                          What life is really for
                          Now I can close the door on yesterday.

A stony-faced Barbara turns away from him so he runs to face her

                          Without you there
                          To show me that you care
                          I know my life is barely worth a crumb
                          My one request
                          Is put me to the test
                          I'll show you that the best is yet to come.

*He offers Barbara the engagement ring but she breaks from Steven and
moves to her mother. Steven drops romantically onto one knee in front
of Barbara*

> Now I've learned
> What my life's about
> Now I'm depending on you
> To straighten my future out
> For with the love we share
> There's nothing that I lack
> So I promise you now there's no need to go
> back.

Barbara has weakened and takes a pace to Steven

Miss Dixon apprehensively re-appears and sees that the situation has improved. She happily beckons the staff who appear from all corners

Mrs Pilsworth	It must be fate
Mr Pilsworth	How long have we to wait
Both	Until the congregation's humming
	Dum, dum-di-dum
Mr Pilsworth	Well who'd've guessed
	He'd stand out from the rest
All	And show us that the best is yet to come

Miss Dixon picks up her office ruler. She scurries DL *across to the other side of Steven and, waving the ruler in front of his eyes, "conducts" everybody singing*

During this, Steven is inadvertently "regressed" and he "walks" off stage UC

All (*except Steven and Barbara; to Steven*) Now you've learned
What your life's about
(*To Barbara*) Now he's depending on you
To straighten his future out
For with the love you share
There's one thing that is clear
This is going to be the wedding of the year!

During the following sequence the "Today" characters stay "frozen" in silhouette

Lights up on Ruby as she enters from DR. *She is still not dressed to go*

Ruby	It's like a flick
	We fell in love so quick
	An' now I'm gonna stick to you like gum

Johnny enters from DR *carrying his hat*

Johnny	So go get dressed
	We'll soon be headin' West
Both	An' then you'll see
	The best is yet to come!

Johnny (*speaking*) You stay in the apartment, sweetheart. I'll get the car. (*He hugs Ruby, sticks the hat on his head, and moves to go*)
Ruby Hurry, baby!
Johnny (*stopping and turning*) I love you, Ruby!

He hurries out UC *through the frozen "Today" characters*

Ruby (*calling after him*) I love you, Johnny!

She exits DR

Bugs and Fingers appear UR *on the platform*

Bugs (*singing; ironic*)	How sad!
Fingers	Too bad!
Both	They finally been had!
Bugs	And now I got them right beneath
	my thumb!
Fingers	It just ain't fair!
Bugs	They think they're free as air!
Both	How could that dopey pair
	Have been so dumb?
Bugs	(Dum Di Dum)
Both	(Dum Di Dum Di Dum Di Dum)
	And now they'll learn the best is
	yet to come!

Bugs whispers in Fingers' ear

Fingers nods and exits

Steven has returned to today. Barbara softens and turns to Steven

Steven } *(to each other)* {   I hardly knew
Barbara   How much I needed you
                                    Until I nearly threw it all away
                                    But then I saw
                                    What life is really for
                                    Now I can close the door on
                                        yesterday

Barbara holds out her hand for the ring. Steven puts the ring on Barbara's finger

All   And now you'll see
                                    How happy we will be
                                    For now there is no reason to be glum
                                    And what is more
                                    Just think of what's in store
                                    The day you hear the organ
                                    Playing Dum Dum Di Dum (Dum Di
                                    Dum Di Dum Di Dum)
                                    Oh yes you've guessed the best is yet to
                                    come!

Just before the final moment in the number. the music stops in mid-phrase. We hear an unnaturally loud knocking on a door

The today characters "freeze"

The Lights pick out Ruby as she rushes in from the bedroom. She is now dressed to leave. She moves UC

Ruby OK Johnny, let's hit the road! (*Stopping and backing away to* DC) Fingers!

After a moment Fingers enters from UC *and moves through the "frozen" today characters to Ruby* DC

Fingers (*smiling*) Hi Ruby, Happy Valentine's Day. (*He holds out the Red Purse to Ruby*)

Dumbly Ruby goes to take it but Fingers lowers the purse and brings up his other hand which is holding his gun. He points it at her head

The today characters unfreeze and sing

All (*include Bugs; except Ruby and Fingers*) The best is yet to come!

Number ends

END OF ACT I

ACT II

SCENE 1

The Building Site. Present Day. Two Weeks Later

It is pouring with rain. The site is completely flattened land with noisy bulldozers and diggers completing the final stages of demolishing what was once a small community. There is a severe foreman together with several busy workmen

Incongruously, stage L, *there is a small but well tended garden surrounding the back door of Mrs Clarke's cottage.* DLC *is a small table and chair*

Jeff, umbrella held aloft, is talking furiously on his mobile phone.

Jeff (*on mobile*) He's supposed to be with me at Mrs Clarke's place! Miss Dixon, I don't care what Mr Tancred's doing, get him out of the office, into his car and over to Datchet right bloody now!

Mrs Clarke, wearing gumboots, an old raincoat and a plastic hat, enters through her garden carrying a tray with lemonade, glasses and a slice of cake

(*With a big smile; seeing Mrs Clarke approaching*) Mrs Clarke! (*He puts his phone away*)
Mrs Clarke (*calling*) There's your lemonade. Home-made! (*She arranges the refreshments on the table*)
Jeff (*smarmy*) Delicious, but you shouldn't have! Allow me. (*He puts the umbrella over her*)
Mrs Clarke No, no, I love the rain. (*She takes the umbrella, lowers it and hands it to a surprised Jeff*)

Jeff then surveys the noisy mayhem as a workman dashes past with a wheelbarrow

Foreman Shift that cement and fast!
Jeff (*to Mrs Clarke; sadly*) Well, what do you make of all this?

Mrs Clarke Marvellous!
Jeff (*surprised*) Marvellous?

No. 11 In The Rain

Mrs Clarke (*singing*)	Isn't it a beautiful day
Jeff	Beautiful?
Mrs Clarke	To be out in the rain!
Jeff	The mud, the stones, the clay —
Mrs Clarke	All sloshing down the drain
Jeff	And workmen drilling —
Mrs Clarke	It's just so thrilling!
	They're digging up the lane
Jeff	It's cold and it's wet
	And it's noisy
Both	And
Mrs Clarke	Yet it's plain
	This'll be a beautiful day
Jeff	I can't say —
Both	— In the rain

Mrs Clarke (*chuckling; speaking*) Well, it's so nice to meet you, face to face, as they say, Mr — er —
Jeff "Walters". But my friends call me "Jeff".
Mrs Clarke Jeff! Lovely! Well, sit yourself down. Home-made cake, Jack.

(*Singing*)	Isn't it a marvellous day?
Builder 1	Isn't it a marvellous day!
Jeff	Well it's hardly serene
Foreman	It's a beautiful day
Mrs Clarke (*introducing the workmen*)	— That's Paddy, Mick and Ray
	They work that big machine
Jeff	The dirt keeps piling
Mrs Clarke	They keep on smiling
Mrs Clarke and Foreman	A truly vibrant scene!
Builder 2	What a beautiful scene
Jeff	Take a look at this lot
Mrs Clarke	Well it's certainly not mundane
	And isn't it a beautiful day?

Jeff (*speaking*) Well...
Foreman (*speaking aggressively in Jeff's face*) It's a beautiful day!

Mrs Clarke (*singing*)   In the rain

Foreman (*speaking*) ...In the rain!
Jeff (*in defeat*) OK.
Mrs Clarke And I want to thank you for all those lovely flowers you
sent me. And the lovely jubbly chocolates! You're a sweetheart, Jack.
Jeff Actually I'm Jeff!
Mrs Clarke (*loudly*) I'll speak up then, Jack.

Jeff (*singing*)   It's raining. It's pouring
Mrs Clarke   It's such a marvellous day

Jeff (*speaking*) Such a marvellous day?!

Mrs Clarke ⎱ (*singing; together*)   Not dreary, not boring
Builders   ⎰   'Cos rain or shine the outlook's
                                              fine
                                          It's such a beautiful day!
Jeff   Such a beautiful day!
Mrs Clarke ⎱ (*together*)
Builders   ⎰   In the rain

Jeff (*speaking*) This is absolutely delicious cake, Mrs Clarke.
Mrs Clarke It's home-made you know. And the lemonade.
Jeff (*with false enthusiasm*) Yummy!

Mrs Clarke (*singing*)   Isn't that a wonderful sight!

Jeff (*speaking*) Isn't what a wonderful sight?

Mrs Clarke (*singing*)   They're building a dream
Builders   We're building a dream!
Mrs Clarke   It doesn't stop at night
All (*except Jeff*)   The noise, the bangs, the steam
Jeff   The mess, the rubble —
Mrs Clarke   It's just no trouble
                                       I specially like the crane
Builders   (Such a beautiful crane!)
Mrs Clarke   I look at that wall
                                       And I think what we all will gain
                                       Every day a beautiful day
Builders   Every day a beautiful day!
All   In the rain

Jeff	It's raining, it's blowing
Mrs Clarke	It's such a wonderful day
Builders	Truly wonderful day!
Mrs Clarke ⎫ *(together)*	Don't care if it's snowing
Foreman ⎭	'Cos rain or hail or windy gale
	It's such a beautiful day!
Builders	Such a beautiful day!
All (*except Jeff*)	In the rain.

Mrs Clarke (*speaking*) Don't you just love the hustle and bustle?

Jeff (*pointedly*) It's a bit — er — noisy, isn't it?

Mrs Clarke Oh, I love the noise. And the company. It's been terribly lonely here since my husband died.

Jeff (*sympathetically*) Yes, of course. And I can see you'll miss all the workmen when the shopping centre is finally completed and your little cottage is totally enveloped by this vast complex.

MrsClarke No! I just think how handy it will be for the shopping, my dear. More lemonade?

Jeff decides to go along with the happy and positive approach to the weather. The Foreman's firm encouragement may have a little to do with Jeff's sudden change of heart

Mrs Clarke ⎫	
Jeff ⎬ (*singing; together*)	It's raining, it's blowing
Foreman ⎭	It's such a wonderful day
Builders	Truly wonderful day
Mrs Clarke ⎫	Don't care if it's snowing
Jeff ⎬ (*together*)	'Cos rain or hail or windy gale
Foreman ⎭	It's still a beautiful day!
Builders	Such a beautiful day!
Mrs Clarke ⎫	
Jeff ⎬ (*together*)	It's raining
Foreman ⎭	
Builders	Raining
Mrs Clarke ⎫	
Jeff ⎬ (*together*)	It's pouring
Foreman ⎭	
Builders	Pouring
Mrs Clarke ⎫	
Jeff ⎬ (*together*)	It's such a marvellous day
Foreman ⎭	

Builders		Simply marvellous day!
Mrs Clarke		
Jeff	(*together*)	Not dreary
Foreman		
Builders		Clearly
Mrs Clarke		
Jeff	(*together*)	Not boring, 'cos
Foreman		
Builders		Not boring
All		Rain or shine the outlook's fine
		It's such a beautiful day!
Builders		Such a beautiful day
All		In the rain!
		(In the rain!)
		In the rain!

End of Number

Mrs Clarke Oh, dear! (*Looking up to the sky*) Look at that! The rain's stopped.

All the workmen look up and complain loudly

Still, they're forecasting more for tomorrow!
Workmen Hooray, yippee, whoopee!
Mrs Clarke (*to Jeff*) You need more lemonade.
Jeff (*rising and taking out his phone; to Mrs Clarke*) If you'll excuse me, I'll just check how Mr Tancred's doing with the traffic. We want to get down to business.
Mrs Clarke No hurry!
Jeff Yes. We want to discuss this little document, don't we? (*He produces a document*)
MrsClarke Whatever you say, Mr — er —
Jeff Walters.
Mrs Clarke "Walters", of course. The brains going. Going? It's gone!
Jeff But I'm Jeff, remember?
Mrs Clarke (*loudly*) Yes, I'll remember! (*To the workmen*) Coffee break, boys! Lemonade! Cake! In the kitchen!
Workmen Hooray, yippee, whoopee!

The Workmen all rush off round the back of the bungalow sweeping a laughing Mrs Clarke off with them

Foreman (*protesting loudly*) Oy! Come back! You've already had a coffee! Hey! You lot!

They've all gone

(*Flatly*) Take five, boys.

He ambles off after them

Jeff has dialled the number and is now seen in a spotlight DL

Jeff (*on mobile*) Has that idiot left the office yet?! ... I told you to tell him to get over to Mrs Clarke's place right bloody now! ...You put me through to him right-a-bloody-way. What the hell do you mean he told you not to disturb him?!

Mr Pilsworth (*off*) What the hell do you mean, you're "leaving the firm"?!

SCENE 2

Steven's Office. Present Day

Lights up on Steven's office DR. *Steven, is happily clearing his desk* DR *and stuffing papers into his briefcase. Mr Pilsworth, looking furious, is standing between Steven and Barbara who is sitting in a chair, looking blank*

Steven As of this afternoon, Sir.

Mr Pilsworth You have called me into your office to tell me ——?!

Steven — to tell you I'm leaving the firm, yes, Sir.

Mr Pilsworth Of all the — ! Who the — ?! How the —?! What the blazes has got into you?!

Steven I believe I've finally acquired the courage of Johnny May, Sir.

Mr Pilsworth (*bewildered*) The courage of —?!

Steven Johnny May. Gangster circa nineteen twenty-nine.

Mr Pilsworth Nineteen twenty-nine?! (*To Barbara*) You said he'd given up all that psycho-babble! (*To Steven*) She said you said — ! (*Stopping*) What the hell has Mr May from nineteen twenty-nine got to do with you leaving the firm?

Steven I now realize what I had to learn from John May. Guts!

Mr Pilsworth (*bemused*) Guts?

Steven Johnny didn't approve of the way Mr Moran operated so, despite the dangers, he quit. I don't approve of the way you operate so —

Mr Pilsworth You don't approve —?!

Steven And furthermore today I intend to offer myself to Mrs Emily Beatrice Clarke as her legal representative.

Mr Pilsworth (*shouting*) Mrs Clarke's legal — Of all the damn, damn —! Barbara! Say something!

Barbara (*flatly*) I pass.

Mr Pilsworth (*to Steven*) And what about my daughter? You're getting married tomorrow!

Steven I've informed Barbara of my decision and after quite a lengthy and heated debate — we've agreed that the situation in no way affects our feelings for one another. I'll see you at the church tomorrow, Mr Pilsworth — that is if you still wish me to attend.

Mr Pilsworth Of course you've got to attend! You're the blasted bridegroom, for God's sake!

Steven Until tomorrow then. Ten-thirty a.m. I believe. If you'll excuse me, Sir, I have to go and introduce myself to my new client. Good morning. Meeting closed. Have a nice day. Busy, busy, busy!

A furious Mr Pilsworth is speechless

Mr Pilsworth Tancred! You're not leaving, you're fired!

Steven (*politely*) Thank you, Sir. I believe that entitles me to six months' redundancy pay. (*He starts to walk out* DR)

Mr Pilsworth nearly explodes

(*Turning*) And by the way, sir, I've quit smoking. I believe you offered a three months' bonus to each of us who did that.

Mr Pilsworth chokes as Steven turns to go

Barbara (*standing up; firmly*) Steven!

Steven stops

(*Melting*) You were magnificent.

He smiles, blows her a kiss and exits DR

Music **No. 11a**

SCENE 3

The Building Site. Present Day

Busy as ever. Jeff is sitting at the table DL looking dejected. Mrs Clarke, who is "nattering" amongst the Workmen, walks down with "Paddy"

Mrs Clarke No Paddy, I insist. You bring over the wife and kids. Have my spare room for a couple of weeks. (*To Jeff; referring to Paddy*) Needs a helping hand.

Jeff looks sick

A car is heard to screech to a halt from OSR

Jeff Well, if it isn't Mr Tancred!!
Mrs Clarke I'll refill the lemonade. (*To the workmen*) Lunch break boys, sandwiches in the garden!
Workmen Hooray, yippy, whoopee!

The Workmen all rush off round the back of the bungalow sweeping a laughing Mrs Clarke off with them

Foreman Oy! It's not lunchtime yet! Hey! Come back! Mrs Clarke! I'm the boss 'ere! Oy!

They've gone

(*Flatly*) Take five, boys.

He ambles off after them

Steven enters from R, pushed on by a furious Jeff

Jeff Where the hell have you been?!
Steven (*happily*) Sorry, Jeff. Had a little business to deal with.
Jeff Are you ready to deal with Mrs Clarke?
Steven Raring to go!
Jeff OK. As you know, since day one I've been giving her the old soft soap. Now, yesterday she agreed to give Pilsworth and Pilsworth her Power of Attorney. Once we've got her signature on this we can conclude the sale of her cottage to Robertson and its bonus time for us. (*He produces the document*)

Steven Brilliant!

Jeff I think it falls into that category. You and I sign it and we'll finalize it with the old duck this afternoon. Right? (*He offers the document to Steven*)

Steven (*smiling*) Wrong! (*He tears the document in half and throws it in the air*)

Jeff (*astounded*) What the bloody hell — ?!

Steven Say "hallo" to Mrs Clarke's lawyer. (*He holds out his hand*)

Jeff (*agog*) Now you definitely have flipped!

Steven (*pressing on*) And I'm asking Mrs Clarke to give *me* her Power of Attorney. (*He produces papers from his pocket and thrusts them at Jeff*)

Jeff (*reading; totally bemused*) "Bugs Moran beats laundering rap" — "Bugs Moran pleads not guilty in — "

Steven Sorry. That's my honeymoon reading. (*Producing papers from his other pocket*) And I assure you Mrs Clarke will not be selling under any circumstances. (*He takes the "Bugs Moran" papers back and hands Jeff the "Power of Attorney" papers*)

Jeff Pilsworth will hit the bloody roof!

Steven (*happily*) He already did.

Jeff What?!

Steven I've realized what I've learnt from nineteen twenty-nine, Jeff. I'm getting out of Pilsworth and Pilsworth just like Johnny May got out of Chicago.

Jeff I don't give a damn about Chicago!

Steven And neither do Johnny and Ruby. It's Valentine's Day! (*Reading*) They're getting away from the murders! (*He throws a paper in the air*)

Chord

Away from the kidnapping! (*He throws another paper in the air*)

Chord

Away from the — (*Stopping and staring at the print-out in his hand; mortified*) Oh — my — God.

Jeff What the hell! What now?

Chord. Throughout the Number Steven gets increasingly distressed

No. 12 The Hit

Steven (*singing*; *reading*) "Chicago, Thursday Feb fourteen nineteen
twenty-nine
Bugs Moran and gang wiped clean
Happy Valentine!" (*He hands the paper to
Jeff*)
Jeff (*reading in his own accent*; *flatly*) "North Street garage, Feb
fourteen
Seven hoodlums died
P'lice chief quoted at the scene
(*In Brooklyn accent*) "This ain't suicide!'" (*He thrusts the paper
back to Steven*)

Steven They were all killed on St. Valentine's Day! February the
fourteenth. The Moran gang massacred in Chicago.
Jeff There's only one massacre going to take place and it's right here on
September the twenty-first.
Steven (*reading*) Picture "Died Aged Twenty-Three Hoodlum Johnny
May" but I am he and he is me and I can't die today!
Jeff It's not today! It was nineteen twenty-nine!
Steven Jeff, I'm one of them. John May!

*Up on the platform we see nineteen twenty-nine Chicago girls reading
the newspapers*

Steven ⎱ (*reading the headlines*; ⎧ "City aghast as hoodlums get
Chicagoans ⎰ *together*) ⎪ blasted out" here in black and
⎨ white is the obit Bugs and his
⎪ Gang went out with a bang, no
⎩ doubt.
Steven (*singing*)   And today —
Chicagoans   Valentine's day –
All (*except Jeff*)   Is the day of the hit

Steven (*speaking*) At the North Street Garage. That's the Gang's
hide-out!
          (*singing*)   I can see it clear as day
                                Crazy I admit
                                Bugs Moran and Johnny May
                                Waiting for the hit
                                Bugs's gang all dead say p'lice
                                Rubbed out of the zone

> But Johnny May won't rest in peace
> If Ruby's left alone!
(*Speaking*) I've got to see Dr Patel!

Steven goes to run off R *but Jeff grabs him*

*The Workmen enter to see what's going on. Two of them pick up the
discarded print-outs and read them*

Jeff You're not going anywhere!
Steven I've got to sort this out!
Jeff This was sorted out years ago. It's history!

All (*except Jeff; singing*)   "Valentine's Day gang blown away — ker
                               pow"
Steven   No this can't be true — it doesn't fit
                         History's got it wrong!
Jeff   You make a move and I'm gonna prove right
                         now that today —
Chicagoans   Valentine's Day —
All (*except Steven*)   Is the day of the Hit!

Steven (*speaking*) Johnny's got the car. They're just about to leave for
   Idaho.
Chicagoans (*singing*)   Valentine's Day poor Johnny May is dead
Steven (*speaking*) No! No! No!
Chicagoans (*singing*)   Bugs and Co. have hit the final pit
Steven (*speaking*) This can't be right!
Jeff (*singing*)   Listen my friend this has to end I said
                         Or today —
Chicagoans   Valentine's Day —
All   — is the day of the Hit!

*Steven hits Jeff but as he goes to leave Jeff leaps at him and grabs him
around the ankles. The Workmen all join in to separate the brawling
pair. Amid much shouting it ends up resembling a rugby scrum*

A girl, Linda, played by the actress who plays Ruby, enters from DR
*and stops as she sees the two combatants and the yelling crowd of
workmen. We haven't yet seen Linda's face. Linda, back to the
audience, surveys the melee*

Linda Hey!

They continue fighting and yelling

    (*Stepping in a pace*) Hey!!

They continue fighting and yelling

    (*Taking another step*) Hey!! (*Finally she crosses in front of them to* LC, *puts her fingers in her mouth and emits a piercing whistle*)

The men all break R

    Anybody here called Tancred? Steven Tancred?!

Steven and Jeff, both breathless, cease their skirmish and turn to face the girl

Steven sees her and stops dead, dumbfounded. "Linda" is "Ruby"!

Music **No. 12a**

The faint "echoing" first phrase of "One of Those Moments" is heard

Steven (*whispering*) Ruby!
Linda What??

Music

The faint "echoing" second phrase of "One of Those Moments" is heard

Steven (*whispering*) Ruby!
Linda Are you Steven Tancred?

Music

The faint "echoing" third phrase of "One of Those Moments" is heard

Steven (*whispering*) Ruby!
Linda (*to Jeff*) Is he Steven Tancred?

Jeff nods. Linda looks back to Steven

Music

The faint "echoing" fourth phrase is heard

During this Linda takes her fist back and delivers a "straight right" to Steven's nose — the "hit" coincides with the last note of the music going very flat. The blow seats Steven in the chair DL. *He just gazes at her while the workmen all react*

Steven (*finally whispering, lovingly*) Ruby!
Linda Now, where's this partner of yours?

Jeff looks worried

Steven Partner?
Linda You both work for Pilsworth and Pilsworth. His name's Jeffrey Walters. He's going to get it, too! (*She furiously raises her fist*)

Behind her back, Jeff rushes off. Linda turns and sees Jeff exit R

(*To Steven*) Was that him?

Steven, still staring at her, can only nod his head

Well, don't worry, your friend Jeff will get his. (*She takes a threatening pace* R)

The Workmen back away

Mrs Clarke appears from her cottage

Mrs Clarke What was all that shouting about? (*Seeing Linda*) What are you doing here, Linda?
Linda (*pointedly*) Introducing myself to Mr Tancred.
Mrs Clarke (*to Steven*) Oh! Your poor nose.
Steven (*grinning*) I'm fine. And — er — "Linda" doesn't have to apologize.
Linda I wasn't going to!
Mrs Clarke (*to the Workmen*) Show's over boys. There's sandwiches to be finished in the kitchen!
Workmen Hooray, yippee, whoopee!

The Workmen rush around the back of the cottage

The Foreman is left alone. He tries to speak, but says nothing

Foreman (*finally; flatly*) Take five, boys.

He ambles off after the Workmen

Mrs Clarke Now, Linda! This gentleman's a lawyer!
Linda I'm well aware of that, Granny! Mr Tancred works for that bastard, Robertson.
Mrs Clarke Hey, language! You're not too old to get a smacked bum, you know.
Steven (*rising; to Linda, amazed*) Are you this lady's granddaughter?
Linda Yes I am and don't think I don't know what you're up to with all the flowers and the soft soap.
Mrs Clarke You're so mistrusting, Linda. (*Crossing to Steven and sitting him down*) She's a good girl, though. Visits her old Granny two times a week. Every Monday, Wednesday and Friday. (*She smiles lovingly at Linda who starts to gently push Mrs Clarke,* SL)
Linda (*firmly*) Granny, why don't you get me a nice glass of your lemonade.
Mrs Clarke Right! And something for that poor nose of yours, Mr — er — er —
Linda Tancred!
Mrs Clarke Of course! I knew it began with a "W". (*To Steven; shouting*) You stay right there, Jack!

She exits into her bungalow

Linda (*angrily*) It's despicable what you're trying to do to that old lady.
Steven (*rising*) Right. And I'm going to fight tooth and nail to save your granny's house.
Linda (*staggered*) I thought you represented that rat, Robertson.
Steven Not any more.
Linda (*thrusting her face into his*) Are you for real?
Steven (*as Johnny*) I sure am, Ruby. (*He is so sure that Linda is Ruby that he gives her a long lingering kiss*)
Linda (*struggling free*) Hey! (*Taking her fist back to strike him again then stopping*) What did you do that for?
Steven (*realizing; aghast*) Oh my God! I kissed you.
Linda I know that! And what's all this "Ruby" business?
Steven (*in one excited breath*) Look, it's difficult to explain but the most amazing thing has happened to me but now it doesn't add up and we've got a problem and somehow or other you must be part of nineteen twenty-nine and the only person who can sort this out is Dr

Patel in Putney!
Linda Wait a minute! Dr Patel?! Putney?! Nineteen twenty-nine?! What
the hell are you talking about?!
Steven Just trust me!

*Linda steps forward and addresses the Audience. During the Number
Steven's desperation and intensity grows as does Linda's determination
to resist — until the last moment*

No. 13 Trust Me

Linda (*singing*)	I'd like to believe him
	But there've been too many men
	Who came by and said
	"Please trust me" — then fled
	So I'm not being stupid again
	Once you hear him say "trust me"
Steven	Trust me!
Linda	With that puppy dog look in his eye
	Then he'll go on to "believe me"
Steven	Believe me!
Linda	And soon there'll be pigs in the sky
	And once he says —

As Steven sings the following line Linda cheekily mimes the words

Steven	I am sure that I met you a lifetime ago
Linda	Why then you're off to a place
	Where the wild geese chase
	"Trust me" — I know!
	Once you hear him say "trust me"
Steven	Trust me!
Linda	With that soppy ol' bambi-eyed look
	Then you're gonna get "I need you"
Steven	I need you
Linda	And then you'll be caught on the hook
	For once he cries —
Both	There is somebody special I want you to meet
Linda	He takes you back to his lair
	And his mother is there!
Both	Trust me
Linda (*ironically*)	How sweet!

	I'd like to believe him
	But I still remember when
	The last wolf came by
	And spun me that lie
	And I nearly wound up in his den!
Linda	Every time he says "trust me"
Steven	Trust me!
Linda	I see shoals of red herrings pass
	Still I wish that I could help him
Steven	Please help me!
Linda	Despite all these snakes in the grass
	For when he says
Both	There is something important we both have
	to do
Linda	Why then it's hard to walk by
	Letting sleeping dogs lie
Steven	Trust me!
Linda	It's true!
	It's the way he says
Steven	Trust me!
Linda	Trust me!
	And I feel my resolve start to ebb
	I'm so tempted to go with him
Steven	Come with me!
Linda	But then I'll be caught in his web
Both	If only just once
	You would shut up and hear what I
	am trying to say!
Linda	Then I might trust you

Steven (*gently putting his hand on her shoulder; simply*) Trust me —
Linda (*speaking*) What the hell! Putney, then!
Both OK!

She grabs his hand and they start to run off

Mrs Clarke arrives with a tray of lemonade, sandwiches and a medical box

Mrs Clarke Hey! You two! Where you off to?!

They stop

Steven Don't give in, Mrs Clarke! And don't sign anything without my

OK!

They run off

Mrs Clarke (*shouting off*) Linda! Your lemonade — sandwiches! Mr
"W"! Your bloody nose!

Sound of car starting up

(*Yelling*) Where are you going?
Linda (*yelling*; *off*) Nineteen twenty-nine! Putney!
Mrs Clarke Nineteen twenty-nine?! Putney? (*To audience*) I hope she
isn't going to be stupid again.

Music **No. 13a**

SCENE 4

Dr Patel's Consulting Room. Present Day

Steven is lying back on the couch DL. *Dr Patel is standing above him,
waving the pendant. Linda is sitting in a chair to the right of the door,
watching in excited amazement*

Dr Patel Listen to my voice Steven. There is nothing but my voice. All
is calm. Calm. Nothing but my voice. Relax, all is calm, calm.
Linda (*standing up*) Is he there yet?
Dr Patel Miss Clarke, please!
Linda We need to know if they made it out of Chicago !
Dr Patel I've told you twice already. You mustn't interrupt. Mr Tancred
is very tense at the moment.
Steven (*sitting up*) I'll relax, I'll get there.
Dr Patel Steven please! Lay back. (*To Linda*) And you really shouldn't
be present during this procedure, Miss Clarke. So! No more
interruptions. Please!

Linda sits

(*Waving his pendant*) Now Steven. Relax. Relax. There is nothing
but my voice. My voice. All is calm. Calm. Calm.

Lights and sound effects

Steven (*happily*) Yes! Yes! Everything's all right. Yes!

Linda (*standing up*) I think he's going!
Dr Patel Sit!

Linda sits

Steven (*as Johnny*) Yeah! Yeah! It's great! I've parked the car! I'm
runnin' up the stairs to the apartment.
Linda (*incredulous*) He's become Johnny May!
Dr Patel Ssh!
Steven (*as Johnny*) I'm pickin' up Ruby! We're headin' for Idaho!
Linda (*ecstatic; standing up*) They're going to make it!
Dr Patel Sit!
Linda The newspapers got it wrong !!
Dr Patel Sit!

Linda does

And stay!

Steven stands up and becomes "Johnny"

Steven (*as Johnny*) I'm so happy, happy, happy! I'm gettin' away with
Ruby, Ruby, Ruby!

Steven turns and walks off stage

Lights and Music whizz us back through time

SCENE 5

Johnny's Chicago apartment. 1929

Johnny (*off*) Ruby! Ruby! Ruby!

Johnny enters

(*Calling out*) Ruby! OK, baby, this is it! (*Moving* DR *to open the
bedroom door*) Car's waitin'! Idaho, here we come!
Fingers Hi, Johnny!

Fingers has stepped out of the darkness behind Johnny and moved DC

Johnny (*stopping dead; trying to be casual*) Hi, Fingers.

Fingers Bugs wants to see you, Johnny, at the garage.

Johnny I'm seein' him later. When we blow away Capone. Yeah. Sure I'll be there tonight.

Fingers (*moving to Johnny* DR; *still smiling*) You're seein' Bugs now, Johnny. And you know what?

Johnny (*nervously*) What?

Fingers Bugs wants to see Ruby, too.

Johnny (*heart sinking; feigning surprise*) Ruby? You mean Bugs' broad, Ruby?

Fingers That's the one, kid.

Johnny (*trying to be casual, moves in front of Fingers to* C) Why would Ruby be — er — what's Ruby got to do with me?

Fingers I figure that's what Bugs wants to know, too. (*He produces Ruby's Red Purse and throws it to Johnny*)

Johnny looks at it with foreboding

(*Taking out his gun and moving to the bedroom door*) OK, Johnny. Here's your Valentine's Day present. (*He opens the bedroom door*)

Fingers throws Ruby into the room

Ruby has her hands tied behind her back and her mouth is gagged

Johnny Ruby! (*He goes to move to her*)

Fingers (*bringing his gun up to Ruby's head*) OK kids. Bugs wants to see you. At the garage. (*He harshly pushes them in front of him and marches them to the door*)

They exit

Fingers (*off; echoing*) ... at the garage... the garage...the garage...

Lights and music **No. 14** *take us back to Today*

Steven (*off*) No, Not the garage! Not the garage!

Dr Patel (*off*) Calm, Steven, calm!

Steven (*off*) But that's where the massacre took place ... the massacre... at the garage...the garage...

Black-out

No. 14 Time's Up

Ensemble (*starting offstage and continuing under dialogue*)
Tick Tock Tick Tock Tick Tock Tick Tock Tick
Tick Tock Tick Tock Tick Tock Tick Tock Tick
Tick Tock Tick Tock Tick
Tick Tock Tick Tock etc.

SCENE 6

The Present Day

A spotlight picks up Jeff on his phone

Jeff (*on mobile*) Barbara! Is that idiot fiancé of yours with you?!

A spotlight picks up Barbara on her phone

Barbara (*on mobile*) I thought he was with you!
Jeff (*on mobile*) Well, he's not!
Barbara (*on mobile*) But it's his stag party, isn't it?
Jeff (*on mobile*) We're all here, he isn't!
Barbara (*on mobile*) Where the hell —? Jeff, you don't think —?
Jeff (*on mobile*) Oh, my God!
Barbara ⎫
Jeff ⎭ (*together; on mobile*) Putney! Time's up!

Lights open up. They put their mobiles away and step to each other

Barbara ⎫ (*singing; together*)   Time's up!
Jeff ⎭   Time to choose
                                      There's no time to lose
                                      Time's up!
                                      Can't you see?
                                      Now our future's in jeopardy

Miss Dixon and the Female Staff enter (with male voices backing from 1929)

Ensemble   Time's up!
Jeff ⎫
Barbara ⎭ (*together*)   There's no going back
Ensemble   Time's up!

Jeff ⎱ (*together*)	Life's a one-way track
Barbara ⎰	
Ensemble	Time's up!
Jeff ⎱ (*together*)	You'll see any day
Barbara ⎰	You're throwing your life away

Ensemble (*under*)   Tick Tock Tick Tock

Jeff ⎱ (*together*)	**Ensemble**
Barbara ⎰	
Choose	Tick Tock Tick Tock Tick
No time to lose	Tick Tock Tick Tock Tick
No going back	Tick Tock Tick Tock Tick
Life's a one-way track	
Choose	Time's up no way back
No time to lose	
No going back	Life's a one-way track
Better follow a diff'rent tack	Soon your nerve will crack
	Better follow a diff'rent tack

Mr Pilsworth appears beside Barbara and Jeff

Mr Pilsworth Gone to Putney again?!! You said he'd stopped all that rubbish!
Barbara I know!
Mr Pilsworth It's supposed to be his stag party!
Barbara I know!
Mr Pilsworth You realize you're marrying this raving idiot tomorrow!
Barbara (*suddenly bursting into tears*) I know! (*She collapses into Jeff's arms*)

Jeff looks vaguely surprised then smiles happily

The Today characters ease into a less prominent position as we segue into next scene

SCENE 7

Interior Garage and Street. 1929

The Gangsters and Bugs in grim silhouette. In the street outside the Young Bum is in his usual position outside the garage DL

*Throughout the scene the 1929 and Today Ensemble sing together. The
Young Bum does not sing*

Mr Pilsworth (*singing*)	Time's up!
All	Now there's no way through
Mr Pilsworth	Time's up!
Bugs	That's the end of you
	Time's up!
All	Things are looking black
	They'll crack when they're on the rack
	Time's up! Tick Tock Tick
	Time's up! Tick Tock Tick time's up!
	Tick Tock Tick time's up.

*Fingers pushes on Johnny and Ruby who is still gagged and bound
from* DR *to* DL *towards the Young Bum*

Fingers Move it!

Johnny	**Ensemble**
(*to Ruby; as they walk*)	Tick Tock Tick Tock Tick Tock
Time has always been my friend	Tick time's up
Ev'ry minute ev'ry hour	Tick Tock Tick Tock Tick
That I spent with you.	Your future's in jeopardy.

Young Bum Hi, Johnny. Can you spare a dime?
Johnny Sure thing, kid. (*He stops and, smiling ruefully, takes out his
wallet and hands the Young Bum a bill*)
Young Bum Wow! Gee, thanks. One whole dollar.
Johnny (*wryly*) Happy Valentine's Day.
Young Bum You betcha!

The Young Bum rushes off

Fingers (*wryly chuckling*) Yeah Happy Valentine's Day! (*Banging on
the garage door*) Hey, open up! It's Fingers!

1st Gangster unbolts the door

Fingers pushes Johnny and Ruby in

Bugs Hey guys. Looks like we got visitors. Come on in, Johnny, my
loyal friend! Hi Ruby, sweetheart.

Fingers undoes Ruby's gag and unties her hands

Bugs	**Ensemble** (*today and 1929*)
Time's up, Ruby doll	Time's up!
My sweet gangster's moll	Tick Tock Tick Tock
And her Johnny May	Tick
Did you think	Time's up!
You could get away?	Tick Tock Tick Tock
	Tick
	Time's up
	Tick Tock Tick
Making me a fool?	Time's up!
Loyalty's my rule	Tick Tock Tick Tock
Know what I should do?	Tick
Make damn certain	Time's up!
Time's up for you	Tick Tock Tick Tock
	Tick
	Time's up
	Tick tock tick

The following four parts are sung together

Barbara }	**Bugs**
Jeff } (*together*)	Time's up, Ruby doll
Mr Pilsworth }	My sweet gangster's moll and
Choose	her Johnny May
No time to lose	Did you think you could get
	away?
No going back	
Life's a one-way track	Making me a fool?
Choose	Loyalty's my rule
No time to lose	
	Know what I should do?
No going back	
Better follow	Make damn certain
A diff'rent tack	Time's up for you!
	Time's up!
Time's up for you	
Time's up!	
Ensemble (*today*)	**Ensemble** (*1929*)
Time's up!	Time's up!

Tick Tock Tick Tock
Tick
Tick time's up!
Tick Tock Tick Tock
Tick
Time's up!
Tick Tock Tick
Time's up!
Tick Tock Tick Tock
Tick
Time's up
Tick Tock Tick Tock
Tick
Time's up
Tick Tock Tick
Tick Tock Tick Tock
Tick Tock Tick
Tick Tock
Tick Tock
Tick
Time's up!

Time's up!
Time to choose
There's no time to lose
Time's up!
Can't you see?
Your future's in jeopardy

Time's up!
No way back
Life's a one-way track
Tick Tock Tick Tock
Tick Tock Tick
Tick Tock
Tick Tock
Tick
Time's up!

Girls (*whispering intermittently under the ensuing dialogue*)
Tick Tock Tick
Time's up

Bugs (*smiling pleasantly*) Hey, Fingers, untie my little girl. (*Falsely welcoming*) Ruby! Johnny! I'm a generous guy — you have two choices. Number one — Johnny stays here and bumps off the Capone mob tonight like we planned — and you (*Pointing to Ruby*) get back to my bed where you belong. All will be forgiven — I'm a generous guy —

Gangsters Yeah! Real generous./ You're the greatest, Bugs!

Bugs Shut up!

Ruby What's the second choice?

Bugs You both get down on your knees, say a little prayer and Fingers will, very sadly, blow your brains out.

One of the Gangsters laughs

Shut up! (*To Johnny and Ruby*) So, what's your choice?

Johnny (*simply*) Mr. Moran — we love each other.

Bugs (*with false emotion*) Ahhh!

Johnny I'm no good to you dead. I'll bump off Mr Capone and his
gang. I'll stay with you and the mob forever. I give you my word — if
you let Ruby go.

Bugs (*sadly*) You missed the point, Johnny. Either she gets back to my
bed or she gets down on her knees.

There is a pause then Ruby sinks to her knees

Johnny (*shattered*) Ruby!

There is a brief moment of tension then Johnny kneels beside her

Bugs (*the hatred coming through*) Well — whad'ya know? (*He looks
to Fingers*)

*Fingers walks over to Johnny and Ruby and raises his gun. Johnny and
Ruby hold hands*

Ruby Goodbye Johnny.

No. 15 One of Those Moments (Reprise)

.

Johnny)   It seems that our dream has been
Ruby)   broken
                                      And true love is destined to die
                                      But if this is the way it must
                                          happen
                                      It's better than living a lie

*Fingers slowly looks to Bugs. Bugs then looks surprised that they
are vocalising when they are about to be shot! Then the surprise
turns to derision at the sentiment of the lyrics and Bugs mimes
"Boo Hoo" tears. He then gets the Gang to join in. And, finally, he
invites the Audience to see the irony*

Johnny   I guess this is one of those
                                          moments
                                      Where the Joe an' the Jane say
                                          goodbye.
Ruby   Yeah, I guess this is one of those
                                          moments
                                      They try not to cry

Johnny }
Ruby   } (*singing*; *together*)   They are both walkin' into the
                                         sunset
                                       With a love that is precious as pearl
                                       Now all that is missin'
                                       From endin's like this

However, the Gang have now become affected by the emotion

Johnny   Is the guy kinda
                                       Kissin' the girl... (*He kisses her*)

And now even Bugs is affected

Ruby   And the girl kinda kissin' the guy
                                       (*She kisses him*)
Johnny   That's the guy who will never say
                                         die
Ruby   We will never say die

End of Number

Bugs pulls himself together

Fingers (*gleefully*) I'm in no hurry, Mr Moran.
Bugs (*smiling thinly*) Any last words, Johnny?
Johnny I love you, Ruby!

Lights and music **No. 15A** *whizz us back through time*

(*Echoing*; *off*) I love you Ruby — Ruby! — Ruby! — I love you
Ruby! — Ruby

Johnny and Ruby have "walked" into next scene

SCENE 8

Dr Patel's Consulting Room. Present Day

*Linda is sitting in the chair upstage by the door. Dr Patel is standing
over Steven who is laying on the couch*

Steven (*as Johnny*; *sitting up and yelling*) I love you, Ruby!

Linda jumps up

Linda Jeez!
Steven I love you, Ruby! (*He falls to his knees at the foot of the couch*)
Dr Patel Calm, Steven, calm.
Linda (*stepping in*) What happened, for God's sake?
Steven (*as Johnny; in tears, grabbing her hands and pulling her down beside him*) I love you, Ruby! (*He takes her face in his hands and kisses her passionately*)

Linda for a moment is motionless — then slowly her arms come up and she holds him tight

I'll love you forever. (*Looking front*) OK, Fingers, we're ready. (*He closes his eyes*)
Dr Patel It's all right. You're back. You're here. You're "Steven". (*He snaps his fingers*)

Steven opens his eyes. He then turns and just stares blankly at Dr Patel for a moment. He then turns to Linda who is totally overcome

Steven The newspapers got it right.
Linda (*hesitating then gently putting her hand on his*) I'm — sorry.

Steven can only nod

You OK?
Steven I'll be fine thanks, Ruby.
Linda (*with a gentle smile*) It's Linda.
Steven (*looking at her; with a gentle smile*) Yes — Linda.

No. 16 This Can't Be Right

Linda	The sound of your voice
	The look in your eye
	The way that you say my name
	It's such a familiar feeling and yet
	How can I recall what I didn't forget?
Linda } (*together*) **Steven**	But this can't be right
	I don't know you at all
	Though it seems like I've known you for

	years
	No this can't be right
	For I cannot recall
	Having met you before tonight.
Linda	This can't be right
Steven	The sound of your voice
Linda	The look in your eye
Steven	The way you sigh
Linda	The way that you say my name
Steven	How strange that it's all just the same
Linda	It's such a familiar...
Steven	It seems so familiar...
Linda	Feeling and yet
Steven	That look on your face
Linda	How can I recall...
Steven	But all ...
Linda	What I didn't...
Steven	So....
Linda	Forget?
Steven	Out of place
Linda ⎱ (*together*) **Steven** ⎰	But this can't be right
	I don't know you at all
	Though it seems like I've known you for years
Linda	No this can't be right
Steven	This can't be right
Linda	For I cannot recall
Steven	Cannot recall
Linda	Having met you before ...
Steven	Having met you
Linda	Tonight
Linda ⎱ (*together*) **Steven** ⎰	This can't be right

Black-out

SCENE 9

The Present Day

On the platform are Barbara, Mr Pilsworth and Jeff

Barbara I'll kill him!
Mr Pilsworth No, I'll kill him!

Jeff Allow me, I'll kill him!

Jeff exits

Music **No. 16a**

SCENE 10

Outside Dr Patel's House. Present day

Linda comes out of the house. She is still in an emotional state, dabbing her eyes with her hanky

As Steven comes out she hastily puts her hanky away. They look at each other awkwardly. Steven takes his handkerchief out and wipes his eyes. He blows his nose then puts his handkerchief away

Steven Look, I made a bit of a fool myself in there. Sorry about that.
Linda No problem. The tranquillisers should kick in about now.
Steven Great. Well — er — thanks for coming with me.
Linda Don't know that I was of any help. Apart from the tranquillisers.
Steven Yes. Well — thanks, anyway.
Linda You've already said that.
Steven I did, didn't I. Right. So — er —
Linda "Thanks", yes. (*Suddenly*) Do you want to go for a cup of tea or something?
Steven (*looking at watch*) That sounds a great — (*Realizing*) Oh, my God! No, I can't. I'm late already. I'd like to see you again, though. May I call you?
Linda (*grinning*) I thought you'd never ask! (*She turns away to scribble her number on a piece of paper*)
Steven It won't be for a couple of weeks. When I'm back from my honeymoon.

Linda stops scribbling. She doesn't know why she's affected by Steven's "honeymoon"

Linda (*off hand*) Honeymoon?
Steven I'm getting married.
Linda That's — great!
Steven Tomorrow, actually.
Linda Wow! Terrific. (*She angrily finishes writing her number and holds out the piece of paper*)

Steven Are you married or anything?
Linda Not even "or anything".
Steven (*taking the piece of paper from her*) Well, I'd better hurry. It's
my stag party tonight.
Linda (*flatly*) Have fun.
Steven I'll drop you off somewhere, shall I?
Linda No, I think I need a bit of private time. Drive carefully.
Steven (*smiling*) See you.
Linda (*smiling*) See you. And — er — good luck for tomorrow.
Steven Yes. "Bye, Ruby".

Steven hurries off DR

Linda (*after a moment, yelling after him*) It's Linda!! (*She turns back
and gives a sad smile*)

No. 17 The Thing About Ruby (Reprise)

(*Singing*)   The thing about Ruby
                          She found the right fella
                          And they've been together ever since
                          The thing about Linda
                          Is this Cinderella
                          Has just found another girl's prince.

She starts to walk off DL

Steven excitedly hurries back on from DR

Steven Linda!
Linda (*stopping but not turning back to him*) Don't tell me. You've run
out of petrol!
Steven No! I suddenly realized!
Linda What?
Steven The newspapers said the massacre was carried out by Capone's
mob — but it was Fingers who was about to blow our brains out!
Linda (*turning to him*) I really think you should get to your stag party.
Steven And Ruby was in the garage with me. None of those newspapers
said anything about a girl among the bodies! I'm missing something.

Jeff hurries in from DR

Jeff Yes! There are thirty guys waiting for you at your stag party! Come
on! (*He grabs Steven*)
Steven I need to sort this out!
Jeff No, you need to stop visiting this shrink! (*He turns Steven to go*)
Steven (*resisting*) Jeff! The newspapers have got it wrong!
Jeff Newspapers always get it wrong! Move it!

Music **No. 18** *starts underneath*

Linda Wait a minute. Who the hell are you?
Jeff Jeff Walters. This idiot's babysitter!
Linda Jeff Walters?!
Steven (*to Linda*) Leave Mr Walters to me.
Jeff (*to Linda*) And who the hell are you?
Linda Mrs Clarke's granddaughter!
Jeff (*amazed*) Mrs Clarke's —?! What the hell are you doing — ?!
You just go home to Granny while she still has a home. Move it! (*He
pushes her away*)

No. 18 Move It

Linda (*to Jeff*)	What d'you think you're doing?
	Don't you give me a shove!
Steven (*to Jeff*)	What d'you think you're up to?
Jeff (*shoving Linda*)	Now the show's over, love!!
Linda	Help! I've been molested!
Jeff	Just do as I requested!
Steven	It's time that I protested —
Linda (*to Steven and Jeff*) Now you two should be arrested!	
Steven	Fool !
Jeff	Jerk !
Linda	You moron!
All	Go on "move it" I said
Steven	Before I see red
Jeff	Oh look! I'm shaking with dread!
Linda (*to Jeff*)	You halfwit!
(*Of Jeff*)	This man's so stupid
	That he must be inbred!
Jeff (*of Linda*)	Soft in the head!
All	Move it I said!

Linda shoves Jeff

Dr Patel hurries out of his house alerted by the noise

Dr Patel (*speaking*) What's going on here?! (*Seeing Jeff*) It's you again
— the madman!
Jeff (*to Linda*) I'm warning you, Miss Clarke! !
Linda (*to Jeff*) No, I'm warning you, you moron! Take that! (*She goes
to punch Jeff*)

Jeff ducks. Linda hits Dr Patel on the chin

(*to Dr Patel*) I'm so sorry, Doctor!

Jeff (*singing; to Linda*)	What d'you think you're doing?
	Are you crazy or what?
Steven	Take your grubby fingers off her, Jeff!
Dr Patel	P'raps I could establish
	If he's crazy or not?
Jeff (*shouting at Steven*)	I told you to move it!
	Are you deaf?!
Linda	You should be admitted!
Dr Patel	If I may be permitted —
Jeff	— Or maybe just slow-witted?!
All (*to the other two*)	Now you should all be committed

Jeff (*to Steven*) Now, move it, Steven!
Dr Patel Stop that! Mr Tancred has just had a very traumatic
experience. He's on tranquillisers!
Jeff He'll need more than tranquillisers when he marries Miss
Pilsworth tomorrow!
Linda (*incredulous*) Wait a minute. He's marrying Pilsworth's daughter?
Jeff (*to Linda*) I told you, go home!
Steven Yes, please go home!
Linda (*now getting emotional*) Why the hell didn't you tell me it was
Pilsworth's daughter? Take that! (*She goes to punch Steven*)

Steven ducks. Linda hits Dr Patel on the chin

Dr Patel (*singing*)	Ouch !
Jeff	Whoops !
Linda (*to Dr Patel*)	I'm sorry!
All	Time to "move it" I think

Dr Patel (*of Jeff*)	He's right on the brink
Linda (*to Dr Patel*)	Oh dear your nose is all pink!
Dr Patel	And puffy!
Jeff (*to Steven*)	Next time think twice
	Before you visit a shrink!
	Or you could soon land in the clink!

Linda (*speaking*) And you wouldn't have got one kiss out of me if I'd known it was Pilsworth's daughter!

Steven I kept thinking you were Ruby.

Jeff Explain later! Now, move it! (*He grabs Steven*)

Steven That's it, take that! (*He takes a swing at Jeff*)

Jeff ducks. Steven hits Dr Patel

Dr Patel Ouch!

Jeff Steven, move it! (*He turns Steven once more*)

Linda Hey, you idiot, take that! (*She grabs Jeff and goes to punch him*)

Jeff ducks. Linda hits Dr Patel again

(*to Steven*) You said "trust me"!

Steven (*to Linda*) You can trust me!

Dr Patel (*pointing at Jeff*) It's that madman's fault. I have been struck once in the eye and three times on the nose!

Linda (*to Steven*) It's a great "come on" isn't it?! "I loved you in nineteen twenty-nine! Kiss me!"

Dr Patel (*singing; to Jeff*)	Fool!
Jeff (*to Dr Patel*)	Quack!
Linda (*to Steven*)	You trickster!
Steven	Now hold onto your hat!
Linda (*to Steven*)	You fast talking rat
	What did you think you were at?!
Steven	I'm sorry!
Jeff (*pushing Steven*)	Don't mind my friend
	He's got the brains of a gnat!
(*To Steven*)	Move it you prat!
Dr Patel	Move it!
Linda	Hold it!
Jeff (*grabbing Steven*)	Shift it!

Steven (*to Jeff*)	Stop it!
Dr Patel (*to Jeff*)	Hold it!
Jeff (*to Dr Patel*)	Stuff it!!!!!
Linda (*to Jeff*)	Shift it!
Steven (*to Linda*)	Drop it!
Linda (*to Steven*)	Hold it!
Jeff (*to Linda*)	Move it!
Dr Patel (*to Jeff*)	Hold it!
Steven (*to Jeff*)	Hop it!
All	Take that!

They all take their fists back to punch and "freeze" in a tableau

A police whistle is heard off L

> *A policeman runs on carrying his baton. He surveys the tableau and blows his whistle again. The tableau comes to life, reacts and rushes off* R *pursued by the policeman*

Music **No. 18a**

Black-out

SCENE 11

Outside The Church. The Following Morning. Present Day

On the upstage platform area, Barbara, in full wedding regalia is on her mobile. Mr Pilsworth is on her right and Mrs Pilsworth is on his right. The two bridesmaids are on Barbara's left

Barbara (*on mobile*) Steven! Where the hell are you? You missed your stag party, you weren't at Dr Patel's. You haven't been at your flat all night. We had a hundred twenty guests at the church this morning and a hundred and five have left already! ...You were arrested?!
Mr Pilsworth Arrested?!

Mrs Pilsworth takes a quick swig from her whisky flask

Barbara (*on mobile*) Causing a riot in Putney?!
Mr Pilsworth A riot in Putney?!

Mrs Pilsworth takes another quick swig

Barbara (*on mobile*) Where the hell are you now?! ... Putney Police Station?!
Mr Pilsworth Putney Police Station?!

Mrs Pilsworth takes another quick swig

Barbara (*on mobile*) Jeff's fault?! ...Dr Patel?! Mrs Clarke's granddaughter —?! ...Well, why the hell didn't you phone last night?!
Mr Pilsworth Why the hell didn't he phone last night?!
Barbara (*to Mr Pilsworth*) The police have only just returned their mobile phones.
Mr Pilsworth And they're supposed to be lawyers for God's sake! (*Grabbing the mobile phone from Barbara; on mobile*) Get your arse over here now, you twit!
Mrs Pilsworth Language, Gregory. (*Taking the mobile phone; on mobile*) Get your sweet little "botty" over here as soon as possilble. (*She offers the mobile to Mr Pilsworth*)

Mr Pilsworth grabs her whisky flask and takes a long swig

Black-out

Music **No. 18b**

SCENE 12

Outside the Police Station. Present Day

Mrs Clarke pushes Linda out from the Police Station to RC *stage*

Mrs Clarke Just get out, girl! (*Calling back in*) Most kind, Sergeant !
Linda Thanks so much for coming to pick me up Granny.
Mrs Clarke You were all very lucky to get let off with just a caution.
Linda (*grinning*) I think the Sergeant finally fell for my soft soap routine.
Mrs Clarke I think he fell for the home-made lemonade and cake I brought.

A dishevelled Jeff pulls out a dishevelled Steven

Jeff is on his mobile phone. Linda turns angrily away from Steven

Jeff (*on mobile*) No, Barbara, please don't hang up! Tell the Vicar we're
on our way! (*Switching off his mobile; to Steven*) Come on! We're an
hour and a half late already! (*He starts to pull Steven* SL)
Mrs Clarke (*to Steven*) I say! You're not getting married looking like
that, are you?
Steven 'Fraid so.
Mrs Clarke If I was the bride I'd say "I don't".
Steven (*moving to Linda*) Linda — I didn't mean to get you involved.
Linda (*staying with her back to him; coldly*) Saturday's my day off
anyway.
Steven And I'm sorry about all that kissing business.
Linda (*turning back and looking him in the eye*) Water under the bridge,
Mr Tancred.
Jeff (*pulling Steven across*) Excuse us! (*Full of charm*) I'm afraid we
have to rush, Mrs Clarke. (*He pushes Steven* L)
Mrs Clarke (*grabbing Jeff; shouting*) No problem, Jack. (*To Linda*)
Poor boy's deaf. I say, Jack! I got those papers your office delivered
to me this morning.
Jeff (*dismissively*) Great.
Steven Papers? What papers?
Jeff (*hastily*) A few formalities. (*Politely*) Excuse us. The groom has a
date. (*He moves in front of Steven and pulls him* L)
Steven (*dragged away; yelling*) Don't sign anything, Mrs Clarke.
Mrs Clarke (*calling back*) I already did. They're at home.
Steven Linda! Get hold of those papers!
Linda I'm doing nothing more for you!
Steven Bring 'em to the church!
Linda Are you deaf?!

Jeff pulls Steven off DL

Steven (*going*) St Mary's! On the hill! Windsor!
Linda (*yelling*) Get lost!!

Dr Patel comes out

Dr Patel That was most rewarding. The Sergeant and two Officers
have booked in for hypnotherapy treatment. So — do you two ladies
require a taxi service?
Mrs Clarke Well, if you're offering, my granddaughter and I would
like to go to St Mary's Church in Windsor via my little cottage in

Datchet.

Linda Granny, I don't want anything to do with that rat, Tancred!

Mrs Clarke (*putting on the sympathy act*) This is for me, though. Your poor Granny. Your poor — old — Granny.

Linda looks up to heaven

(*to Dr Patel*) Well, if you're sure it's no trouble to give us a lift.

Dr Patel No trouble at all, dear lady. (*He offers an arm to Mrs Clarke*)

Mrs Clarke How very kind. And what's your name, young man?

Dr Patel Dr Patel.

Mrs Clarke Oh, I'll never remember that. I'll call you Petal. (*She takes his arm*)

Dr Patel starts to lead her off DL

(*Stopping and turning to Linda*) I think I've found myself a toy-boy!

They exit DL. *Linda shakes her head and follows them off*

Music **No. 18c**

SCENE 13

Inside the Church. Present Day

There is a centre aisle leading up to the main door of the church and a side aisle from DR *to* UR. *The few remaining guests are sitting in the pews* DRC *in various states of boredom — playing cards, speaking on a mobile, knitting etc.*

Mr Robertson is looking very impatient. He and Mr Pilsworth are having a heated discussion by the altar DL *with Barbara standing there, deadpan, in her wedding dress*

Mrs Pilsworth is sitting in the front pew, half asleep. She is clutching her whisky flask and drinking

On the Platform we see the organist, Mrs Barber, with the organ behind her. Below her, is the Vicar (back to the audience!) who is attempting to placate an angry Mrs Barber. The Bridesmaids hurry in from the side aisle, above the pews to UC

1st Bridesmaid Not a sign of either of them!
2nd Bridesmaid I've got to go. I've got a date!
1st Bridesmaid (*grabbing the 2nd Bridesmaid*) He'll be here.
Mr Robertson Pilsworth, I'm a very busy man!
Mr Pilsworth I do apologize, Mr Robertson.

A dishevelled Jeff bursts through the side aisle UR *and runs to* DR

Jeff OK, OK! He's here!

A dishevelled Steven comes through the aisle UR *and moves* DR *to Jeff's left*

Everyone reacts to the scruffy appearance of the groom. There is a murmur from all followed by a silence

Steven (*weakly*) Morning, everybody. (*Moving to Barbara at* DLC *and just standing there*) Hi, Barbara.
Barbara (*fighting back her tears; wryly*) What do they say about the happiest day of your life?
Steven The day's still young. (*He holds out his hand*)

Barbara hesitates and then takes it

Vicar (*appearing from upstage between Steven and Barbara*) You had us really worried, Mr Tancred.

Steven turns to see the Vicar — it is Fingers! The Vicar is even nearsighted like Fingers and wears glasses. Steven is transfixed

Quick off-key musical chord **No.18d**

Steven (*stepping back a pace* R; *pointing at the Vicar*) Oh, my God!
Vicar (*attempting a joke*) No, just the Vicar.
Mr Robertson (*stepping down beside the Vicar; angrily*) Can we get on with this!

There is another chord as Steven sees Mr Robertson standing next to the Vicar

Steven (*pointing to them both*) You're together again!! (*Backing away* DR) Ooh! Oooh!! Ooooh!!!

Jeff (*grabbing Steven*) Steven!

Mr Robertson looks to the Vicar who is as confused as Mr Robertson

Vicar (*calling*) Now! The bride and bride's father outside, please. Enter on music cue.

Mr Pilsworth and Barbara exit up the centre aisle

(*Calling up*) Mrs Barber, stand by for music!
Mrs Barber (*calling down*) I've been "standing by" for an hour and forty-five minutes!
Steven (*to Jeff*) The Vicar is Fingers!
Jeff (*almost crazed*) The Vicar is the Vicar!
Steven And he's with Bugs!
Jeff (*even more crazed*) No! He's with our bonus!! (*Approaching the sleeping Mrs Pilsworth*) Mrs Pilsworth, I think we're about to start. Mrs Pilsworth — !

Jeff gives Mrs Pilsworth a gentle shake and she wakes with a start

Mrs Pilsworth (*taking his hand; lovingly*) I do, I do!

Linda, Mrs Clarke and Dr Patel enter from the side aisle UR *and walk to* DR

Vicar (*calling up*) Go music! Mrs Barber!
Mrs Barber And about time, Vicar!!

Music **No. 18e**

Mrs Barber starts to play "Here Comes The Bride" at rather a speedy tempo

Vicar Mrs Barber!

Mrs Barber slows the tempo

Jeff (*to Steven*) This is it!
Steven (*to Jeff; whispering urgently*) It must mean something! Bugs Moran and Fingers being at my wedding!!
Jeff (*whispering urgently*) Shut up!!!

Mr Pilsworth and Barbara enter from UC *and walk down the aisle to* DLC

Jeff pushes Steven into his place DLC

The Vicar returns with his prayer book to left of Steven

Jeff gives Mr Pilsworth and Barbara a huge smile as they arrive beside them. Steven tries to give a huge smile. Mr Pilsworth "delivers" Barbara to Steven's right then steps back. The Vicar smiles happily at everyone and removes his glasses. He waves the glasses to and fro as he speaks!

Vicar Now, Steven! Do you understand the meaning of the vows you are about to undertake?

Regression music **No. 18f** *underneath*

Steven looks blankly at the Vicar as Steven starts to get mesmerised by the glasses flicking across his face

Steven?
Steven I — I — I — I —

The Congregation react nervously

Vicar (*nervously waving his glasses*) Do you understand the vows, Steven?

Regression music

Steven I — I — I — I
Vicar (*trying to be calm*) I'm in no hurry, Steven.
Fingers (*off; echoing*) I'm in no hurry, Mr. Moran.

All the Characters "walk" into 1929 as the sound and Lighting whizz us back through time. The female ensemble and stage management remove the pews

Fingers } (*together*) { No hurry, Mr Moran, Mr Moran, Mr Moran.
Vicar } { No hurry, Steven, Steven, Steven.

Inside Garage. 1929

Johnny and Ruby kneeling. Fingers has his gun to their heads. Bugs and the Gangsters are watching in silence

Fingers (*gleefully*) I'm in no hurry, Mr Moran.
Bugs Any last words, Johnny?
Johnny I love you, Ruby.

She gives a brave smile. They close their eyes. Fingers starts to squeeze the trigger. The Young Bum runs into the alleyway from UL *and urgently bangs on the metal door of the garage —* Bang *—* Bang *—* Bang

Johnny ⎫
Ruby ⎬ (*together; yelling*) Ahhh!

After a moment they open their eyes and look at one another — they're still alive!

The Young Bum repeats the urgent knocking — Bang *—* Bang *—* Bang

Young Bum (*off*) Hey! Open the door!
Bugs OK. Let the kid in.

One of the Gangsters does so

The Young Bum bursts in

Young Bum A squad car! And a couple of cops!

The Gangsters hesitate and then quickly take out their shooters and tommy-guns

Bugs Hold it. We ain't doin' nothin' illegal. Just waitin' for a business meeting. Easy, boys! Lose the hardware. We'll get rid of the cops, then we'll get rid of these two, then we'll get rid of Mr Capone!

The Gangsters throw their shooters and tommy-guns into the pile of old tyres. Fingers keeps his gun pointing at Johnny and Ruby

Open up the store room for these two. (*To Johnny*) Just a slight deferment, Johnny.

One of the Gangsters unbolts the storeroom door

Fingers (*to Ruby*) Get in there! (*He throws her into the storeroom*)
Johnny (*turning to the Young Bum and taking out his wallet*) Thanks
for the few extra minutes, kid. Here, take two bucks.
Young Bum Gee, thanks! Thanks! Ma will think it's Christmas!
Johnny What the hell. Take the whole damn wallet! (*He throws his
wallet to the Young Bum*)
Young Bum (*amazed*) But Mister, there's twenty bucks here, and a
driver's licence.
Johnny (*wryly*) There ain't no cars where I'm going.
Young Bum You'll go to heaven, Mister.
Bugs I wouldn't bet on it, kid. Fingers! (*He throws Johnny across to
Fingers*)

There is a banging on the garage door

1st Cop (*off*) Open up in there! This is the police!
Fingers Get in there! (*He pushes Johnny into the storeroom and bolts
the door*)

More banging from outside

1st Cop (*off*) Hey! Open up in there!
Bugs OK. Let 'em in. (*He indicates for the 1st Gangster to open up*)
1st Gangster OK, OK! (*He unbolts the garage door*)

*A Cop enters and a Sergeant follows. The Sergeant remains in the
background*

1st Cop Who's the owner of this garage?
Bugs (*stepping forward*) What's the problem, Officer?
1st Cop Are you Mr Moran?
Bugs Yeah.
1st Cop OK. All of you — up against the wall.
Fingers (*belligerently*) We ain't doing nothin' wrong!
Bugs Cool it. Do as the officer says. OK! Fingers! All of you. Face
the wall.
1st Cop Hands in the air.
Bugs We're clean, Officer.
1st Cop In the air!
Bugs (*overly polite*) Sure, sure. (*He joins the rest of the mob facing the
back wall, hands in the air*)

The Young Bum starts to sidle away

1st Cop Hey! You! Against the wall.
Young Bum I ain't nothin' to do with these guys!
1st Cop Against the wall!
Young Bum Ask Mr Moran! I ain't nothin' ——
1st Cop Against the wall! (*He throws the Young Bum into the line-up*)
Bugs (*calling out*) It's just a board meeting we're having, Officer.(*To Fingers*) Don't forget to "minute" this, Fingers.

The Sergeant, who has stayed in the background, steps down. The Sergeant and the Cop open up their police coats — to reveal tommy-guns

Sergeant (*grinning*) Oh, we'll minute this, Bugs!
Bugs (*turning, horrified; recognizing the voice*) Al Capone!

All the Gangsters turn in terror

Gangsters Al Capone!!!
Sergeant Yeah. Ever - lovin' Al!

The "Cops" let loose a horrendous fusillade of bullets — left and right along the line of defenceless hoodlums. Screams and writhing bodies are everywhere

> *Fingers is "blown" off-stage — to facilitate quick change back to Vicar!*

Al surveys the grim sight

Al Happy St. Valentine's Day, boys.

No. 19 Rat-A-Tat Rag (Reprise)

Al
Cop } (*together*)

Pitter pat start tappin' those feet
It's music time again
Rat-Ta-Tat who's takin' the heat?
It's Bug's merry men
We gonna make a big noise now
We got this town in the bag

You'll see Capone an' his dancin' boys
now

Doin' the Rat-a-Tat rag

Dance break

Al   You'll see Moran lookin' swell there
Cop   Down at the morgue with a tag
                          All of his gang will be down in hell yeah
                          Doin' the Rat-a-Tat

Tap break

Al   You dirty Rat-a-Tat

Tap break

Doin' the Rat-a-Tat rag!

They dance off

There is a pause and then the storeroom door is barged open, splinter-ing the lock

  Johnny and Ruby stumble out

They survey the bloody scene and walk around the gruesome sight in awe. Johnny sees the Young Bum laying dead

Johnny Oh my God!
Ruby My God! (*She clutches Johnny*)
Johnny Well God must have had a hand in it somewhere. (*Grabbing her in an embrace*) Ruby!

The sound of an approaching police siren is heard from off L

Ruby The cops!
Johnny Let's get the hell out of here! (*He pulls her towards the metal door*)
Ruby (*stopping*) Johnny, we'll run right into them. The window! Come on!

Johnny bolts the metal door. Ruby grabs Johnny's arm

Johnny (*stopping*) I gave the kid my wallet! It's got everything in it!

With the sound of the siren getting horribly loud, Johnny moves towards the body of the Young Bum. The siren stops and a police car is heard screeching to a halt

Ruby (*pulling him away*) The papers for the farm are in the car. That's all we need! Come on, the window!

Two cops rush on from UL *and urgently bang on the garage door. Johnny and Ruby freeze*

Young Cop Open up in there! This is the police!

Johnny hesitates for a moment then grabs Ruby and they clamber up the pile of tyres to the window

Come on! Open up!

Johnny breaks the window

Johnny pushes Ruby out

More banging. The young cop starts to barge the door. Johnny is struggling to get out of the window. As the garage door is kicked open Johnny disappears through the window

The two cops burst in. The young cop stops dead at the grizzly sight

Jeez! Mother of God!
Other Cop (*to the Young Cop*) Welcome to Chicago! OK. Check 'em out for identification. Start with that young kid there.

The Young Cop kneels beside the dead Young Bum and removes the wallet from his hand. The Other Cop takes out his notepad

Young Cop Nothin' much on him. Wallet. Few dollars. Driver's licence —
Other Cop Just gimmee the name.
Young Cop (*reading*) John William May.
Other Cop (*writing*) John William May.
Young Cop Born January, twenty-first, nineteen-o-six (*Surveying the mutilated body of Young Bum; to the Other cop*) And died St. Valentine's Day, nineteen twenty-nine.
Other Cop It was a terrible short life —

The words become an echo

(*Echoing*) — a terrible short life —

Music

SCENE 15

Inside the Church. Present Day

As before. Everybody has returned to their positions and the pews replaced

Other Cop (*off; echoing*) — terrible short life... terrible short life... terrible short life...
Vicar — a wonderful long life. A wonderful long life. And now, Steven — Barbara —

To everyone's amazement, Steven, with tearful emotion, drops to his knees

(*Surprised*) Steven?
Steven (*suddenly*) It's OK! It's OK!
Vicar Thank heavens for that ! We'll cut to the end! If anybody here knows of any just cause or impediment —
Steven (*turning to the congregation*) It's OK!!
Mrs Pilsworth (*happily*) It's OK! (*She drinks*)

The guests start to look uncomfortable

Steven (*running* DR *to Linda and grasping her hands*) The newspapers got it wrong, Ruby!
Barbara Ruby?
Congregation Ruby?

General consternation

Linda (*awkwardly; to everyone*) Actually, the name's Linda. (*To Steven*) I think it's time to say "I do".
Barbara What the hell's going on now?! (*She furiously throws her bouquet over her shoulder*)

General consternation

Vicar Miss Pilsworth, we are in Church!

Barbara (*pressing on*; *indicating Linda*) And why the hell are you calling her "Ruby"?!

Vicar Language, please!

Jeff She's Mrs Clarke's granddaughter.

Barbara Mrs Clarke's — ?!

Mrs Clarke (*stepping in*) And she's lovely too!

Linda Granny, please!

Mr Pilsworth (*stepping down*) What the blazes are you two doing at my daughter's wedding?!

Mrs Clarke (*crossing Linda to Mr Pilsworth*) What the blazes are you doing shouting at me and my granddaughter?

Dr Patel (*crossing to Mrs Clarke*) Mrs Clarke, please pipe down!

Vicar Could we all just remember where we are, please?!

Mr Robertson (*pointing to Mrs Clarke*; *furious*) Are you the old bag we're trying to evict?!

Vicar (*yelling*) Please!

Mrs Clarke Yes I am! And not so much of the "old", if you don't mind.

Steven (*earnestly*) Barbara, please! I know what it's all been about now!

Barbara Well nobody else damn well does!

Congregation reacts

Vicar Miss Pilsworth!

Mr Pilsworth If he starts with his ethics, morals, decency!

Steven Yes it's about that but much more. (*To Dr Patel*) I got the final message, Doctor.

Dr Patel And what's that, Steven?

Steven Love. True love conquers anything. (*To Barbara*) Do you love me, Barbara? Do you really love me?

Barbara What the hell do you think I'm doing here?!

Vicar Please!

Linda (*angrily crossing to Barbara*) For God's sake just answer the question!

Congregation Ooo!

No. 20 Tell Him

Linda (*speaking*) Go on!
            (*singing*)   Tell him!

Barbara (*speaking*)What?
Linda (*singing*)   Say what he wants to hear
Barbara (*speaking*) I beg your pardon?
Linda (*singing*)   Why don't you make it clear?
Barbara (*speaking*) Why don't you sit down?
Linda (*singing*)   We haven't got all year!
Barbara (*speaking*) Or just go home!
Linda (*singing*)   Why don't you take his hand and
                                          tell him?
Barbara (*speaking*) Steven, what is going on?
Linda (*singing*)   Tell him your love is real
Barbara (*speaking*) What the hell!
Vicar Please!
Linda (*singing*)   Tell him just how you feel
Vicar Ladies!
Linda (*singing*)   Is it that big a deal?
Steven Barbara?
Barbara (*turning angrily to Linda; singing*) I don't need your
                                          intervention
                                          On my wedding day
                                          Now getting married's my
                                          intention
                                          So let's not delay that OK?!
Linda   No you have to tell him

The Congregation, except Mrs Pilsworth, jump up

Congregation   Tell him!
Linda   } (*together*)   Tell him your heart's desire
Congregation   }
Congregation   Tell him!
Mr Pilsworth   Tell him we've paid the choir!
Mr Robertson   Then we can all retire!
Mrs Pilsworth (*standing; to both*) Shush! (*She falls back into her
   seat*)
Linda (*singing*)   You know he really needs an
                                          answer
Congregation   Answer!
Linda   He can depend upon
Congregation (*standing on their pews*) Tell him!
Mr Pilsworth   We really must get on
Congregation (*pointing their fingers angrily*) Tell him!
Mr Robertson (*looking at his watch*) Another morning gone!

Mrs Pilsworth (*standing up unsteadily*) For heaven's sake Barbara.
  Tell him you love him!

Barbara (*to Steven*)   Do you have to ask me even?
                                              Can't you make a guess?
                                              If I didn't love you Steven
                                              I'd've burnt the dress!
Linda   That's a yes!

The Congregation all sit

Mr Pilsworth (*speaking*) Now if we can just get on with the
  ceremony —
Steven Wait! There's one last question.
Congregation (*rising*) Oh, God!
Vicar Please!
Barbara OK! One last question.
Congregation Oh God!
Vicar Please!!

*Steven pulls a surprised Vicar to him. He then thrusts the Vicar's hand
across him to Barbara's head*

Steven (*to Barbara*) Fingers has a gun to your head — !

For a moment Barbara and the Vicar are mesmerised

Barbara What the hell now?
Congregation Yes, what the hell now?!
Vicar Yes, what the hell now?! (*Realizing what he has said, he claps his
  hand to his mouth and nervously steps back*)

Pause

Steven Would we be prepared to die for one another?

Barbara can only look at him

Linda Go on!
Mrs Clarke Yes, go on!
Linda (*singing*)   Now's the time to tell him
Mrs Clarke   Tell him!!!!!
Linda   Look him straight in the eye
Dr Patel   Tell him!

Linda	Say you're prepared to die
Mr Pilsworth	Tell him!
All (*except Steven and Barbara*)	Don't let the chance go by!
Mrs Pilsworth	For if you really love him
Congregation	Tell him!
Mrs Pilsworth	You shouldn't hesitate
Congregation	Tell him!
Mr Pilsworth	You mustn't make him wait
Congregation	Tell him!

Mr Robertson (*finally getting caught up*) We need to know his fate!

Barbara (*simply*; *speaking*) I don't know if I'd be prepared to die for you, Steven. But I tell you one thing I've learned from nineteen twenty-nine — there's no way I can live with you.

Congregation ⎫
Vicar ⎭ (*together*) Oh, God!

The Congregation turn and furiously start to exit UC *and* UR *with Mr Pilsworth and the Vicar angrily arguing as they follow behind. Mrs Pilsworth staggers after them happily drinking from her flask. Mrs Barber plays a couple of bars of* "Colonel Bogey" *then angrily exits*

Mr Robertson storms past Mrs Clarke

Mrs Clarke (*stopping Mr Robertson*) Hey! Here's your signed papers for you. (*She throws the torn up contract in the air over Mr Robertson's head like confetti*)

Mr Robertson (*ominously*) I could get ugly.

Mrs Clarke You've already arrived.

Mr Roberston reacts angrily and exits

By now everyone has exited except Steven, Barbara, Jeff, Mrs Clarke and Dr Patel

Barbara (*taking Steven's hand and looks at him*) What you're searching for I can't give you. What I want from life — you don't. (*Kissing him gently on the cheek*) And if I asked you the same question, Steven?

Steven (*gently*) I thought I loved you. I really did.

Barbara Almost perfect. (*Smiling*) Great while it lasted. (*She steps back to find herself beside Jeff*)

Jeff (*smiling*) A very wise decision, Barbara. (*He slips his arm around her shoulder*)

They exit UC

Steven (*giving an embarrassed smile and starting to move* UC *but stopping*) I'll see you very soon, Mrs Clarke.
Mrs Clarke And I'll tell you something. If every bride and groom was asked that question of yours there'd be a lot fewer divorces.
Steven (*turning to Linda*) 'Bye, Linda.
Linda (*briefly*) Yeah, 'bye. (*She turns away*)
Steven (*hesitating; turning to Dr Patel*) Good-bye, Doctor. (*He turns and starts to move* UC)
Dr Patel Steven —!

Steven stops

There's one more thing you have to learn from the past.
Steven (*turning*) No! I shouldn't have gone there. (*Emotionally*) You shouldn't have taken me there.
Dr Patel (*smiling*) Don't you know yet what Johnny and Ruby have been trying to tell you. About love.
Steven No! *You* tell me!

Dr Patel goes to speak

> Come on, wise guy, tell me!
> What does this Johnny May
> Have in his heart to say
> Relevant for today?

Dr Patel goes to speak

> I want to know so tell me!
> Does Ruby's point of view
> Offer a vital clue
> Telling me what to do?

Dr Patel goes to speak

> For me the past has been deleted
> Are you not aware?
> That love of ours can never be
>   repeated
> No one could compare

Dr Patel (*indicating Linda; speaking*) She's standing there .

Linda turns and, expressionless, she looks to Steven. She then turns back to Dr Patel and Mrs Clarke. Mrs Clarke smiles and flicks her head in Steven's direction. Linda hesitates then looks slowly back to Steven. Steven, almost as bemused as Linda, slowly holds out his hand to her

Linda (*to Dr Patel and Mrs Clarke; tersely*) What am I to tell him?
Is this what I deserve
Treating me as reserve?
You've really got a nerve!
If you think come what may
I'd give my life away
For someone I've known a day
Here's what I'd have to say —

(*Turning to Steven, softening; surprised, but with feeling*) OK!

Steven smiles happily and opens his arms and Linda jumps up into an embrace

Dr Patel and Mrs Clarke smile and exit

Steven breaks the embrace and starts to pull Linda DL

(*stopping*) Where are we going?
Steven Who knows? Maybe a farm somewhere. (*He takes her hand and starts to run off* DL)
Linda (*stopping*) This is madness! We hardly know each other!
Steven Since nineteen twenty-nine, Linda!

They laugh and run off DL

Remaining principals and ensemble enter and sing

No. 21 Two Of Those Moments

Full Company   At last we have come to that moment
When the past and the present are one
Oh yes, we have come to that moment
Our story is done
The guy and the girl and the love song
And the sun shining bright in the sky
There's nothing that's missing

Steven (double) and Linda (double) excitedly run on from DR *with their
backs to the Audience and point up to the sky and wave*

>From moments like this
>When the gal fin'lly kisses the guy

*Lights come up on the platform area. We see Johnny (wearing his hat)
and Ruby standing there embracing. They break the embrace. The whole
company has now turned up-stage and is waving at Johnny and Ruby
who wave back. Ruby takes the 1929 hat off Johnny's head and throws it
down to Steven (double) who catches it. Steven (double) laughing, sticks
the hat on Linda (double). They embrace*

Ruby (*to Johnny; laughing*) Do you reckon it's OK to have two happy
endings in one story?
Johnny You betcha, baby!

They embrace and run off L

Lights fade out on platform

*During the following Steven and Linda, (cleverly masked by the
company!) replace the embracing Steven (double) and Linda (double).
Steven and Linda break their embrace, face front, and join in the number
at "*Every word that we say seems to rhyme*"*

Guys	It happens just once in a lifetime
Gals	Oh once in a lifetime
Guys	That true love is given to you
Gals	Oh so true
Guys	You'd settle for once in a lifetime
Gals	Once in a lifetime
Guys	But that one time
All	Became two
	The guy and the gal in Chicago
	That couple who ain't got a dime
	They found their true way
	Like our lovers today
	Now the bells shout hooray when
	they chime
	Ev'ry word that we say seems to
	rhyme

> Not once
> But twice upon a time

End of number

CURTAIN

FURNITURE AND PROPERTY LIST

ACT I

SCENE 1

On stage:	Chairs White towels
Off stage:	Truncheon (**Policeman**) Tommy-gun (**Fingers**)
Personal:	**Johnny**: cigarette **Fingers**: spectacles

SCENE 2

Set:	Couch
Strike:	Chairs White towels
Off stage:	Pendant (**Dr Patel**)

SCENE 3

Set:	Desk. *On it:* letters, gold-plated letter-opener, file Chairs
Strike:	Couch
Off stage:	Note (**Miss Dixon**)
Personal:	**Miss Dixon**: watch **Steven**: cigarette **Barbara**: watch **Mr Pilsworth**: watch

SCENE 4

Set:	Tables. *On it:* drinks Chairs

Strike: Desk
                 Chairs

Off stage: A piece of paper (**A gangster**)
                 Gun (**Fingers**)
                 Glass (**A customer**)
                 Red Purse (**Ruby**)

Personal: **Johnny**: cigarette
                 Bugs: cigar

SCENE 5

Set: Bench

Strike: Tables and chairs

SCENE 6

Set: Desk
                 Chairs

Strike: Bench

Off stage: Letter-opener (**Mr Pilsworth**)
                 Tray of coffee (**Miss Dixon**)

SCENE 7

Set: Bench

Strike: Desk and chairs

Off stage: Sandwich (**Barbara**)

Personal: **Barbara**: mobile phone
                 Steven: cigarette

SCENE 8

Set: Couch

Strike: Bench

Off stage: Pendant (**Dr Patel**)

SCENE 9

Set:	Small table Chair. *On it:* Ruby's Red Purse
Strike:	Couch
Off stage:	Red Purse. *In it:* packet of cigarettes (**Ruby**)

SCENE 10

Set:	Pile of old tyres
Strike:	Table and chair
Off stage:	Ruby's Red Purse (**Fingers**) Tommy-guns (**Bugs & Gangsters**) Wallet. *In it:* dollar bill (**Johnny**)

SCENE 11

Set:	Couch
Strike:	Pile of tyres

SCENE 12

Set:	Large table. *On it:* examples of the wedding feast, six-tiered wedding cake, ladle Table. *On it:* three open champagne bottles in ice buckets
Strike:	Couch
Personal:	**Barbara**: watch

SCENE 13

Set:	Table Chair
Strike:	Tables of wedding feast
Off stage:	Small suitcase (**Johnny**) Cigarette and packet of cigarettes (**Barbara**)

SCENE 14

Set: Wedding feast tables

Strike: Table and chair

SCENE 15

Set: Desk. *On it:* a pile of print-outs, ruler

Strike: Wedding feast tables

Off stage: Hat (**Johnny**)
                Ruby's Red Purse, gun (**Fingers**)

Personal: **Barbara**: engagement ring

ACT II

SCENE 1

On stage: Small table
                Chair

Off stage: A tray of lemonade, glasses and a slice of cake (**Mrs Clarke**)
                Wheelbarrow (**Workman**)
                Umberella, document (**Jeff**)

Personal: **Jeff**: mobile phone

SCENE 2

Set: Desk. *On it:* papers
                Office chair

Strike: Small table
                Chair

Off stage: Briefcase (**Steven**)

SCENE 3

Set: Table
                Chair

| *Strike*: | Desk |
| | Office chair |

Off stage: Tray. *On it:* lemonade, sandwiches, a medical box (**Mrs Clarke**)
Document (**Jeff**)
"Bugs Moran" papers, "Power of Attorney" papers (**Steven**)
Newspapers (**Chicago girls**)

SCENE 4

| *Set*: | Couch |
| | Chair |

| *Strike*: | Table |
| | Chair |

Off stage: Pendant (**Dr Patel**)

SCENE 5

| *Set*: | Small table |
| | Chair |

Strike: Couch

Off stage: Red Purse, gun (**Fingers**)

SCENE 6

| *Strike*: | Small table |
| | chair |

Personal: **Jeff**: mobile phone
Barbara: mobile phone

SCENE 7

Off stage: Wallet. *In it:* a dollar bill (**Johnny**)
Gun (**Fingers**)

SCENE 8

| *Set*: | Chair |
| | Couch |

SCENE 9

Strike: Chair
                Couch

SCENE 10

Off stage: Baton (**Policeman**)
                A piece of paper (**Linda**)

Personal: **Steven**: handkerchief, watch

SCENE 11

Off stage: Whisky flask (**Mrs Pilsworth**)

Personal: **Barbara**: mobile phone

SCENE 12

Personal: **Jeff**: mobile phone

SCENE 13

Set: Pews
                Altar
                Organ

Off stage: Whisky flask (**Mrs Pilsworth**)
                Playing cards, mobile phones, knitting etc. (**Guests**)

Personal: **Vicar**: glasses

SCENE 14

Set: Piles of old tyres

Strike: Pews
                Altar
                Organ
Off stage: Whisky flask (**Mrs Pilsworth**)
                Gun (**Fingers**)
                Wallet (**Johnny**)
                Notepad, pen (**Other Cop**)

SCENE 15

Set: Pews

Strike: Piles of tyres

Off stage: Whisky flask (**Mrs Pilsworth**)
                Contract papers (**Mrs Clarkes**)

LIGHTING PLOT

Practical fitting required: nil
Various interior and exterior settings

ACT I, Scene 1

To open: Street lights

No cues

ACT I, Scene 2

To open: General interior lighting

Cue 1	**Johnny**: "Ahhhh!"	(Page 2)
	Light effects	

ACT I, Scene 3

To open: General interior lighting

Cue 2	**Mr Pilsworth**: "Have you got that, Steven?"	(Page 14)
	Light effects	

ACT I, Scene 4

To open: Spotlight on Johnny and Fingers

Cue 3	**Johnny** is smoking a cigarette	(Page 14)
	Lighting opens up	

ACT I, Scene 5

To open: Night time. Twinkling lights are in the backdrop

Cue 4	**Johnny** (*singing*): "To gently caressin' the —"	(Page 24)
	Lighting changes	

ACT I, Scene 6

To open: General interior lighting

No cues

ACT I, Scene 7

To open: General lighting

No cues

ACT I, Scene 8

To open: General interior lighting

No cues

ACT I, Scene 9

To open: General interior lighting

| *Cue* 5 | **Fingers** puts the Red Purse in his overcoat pocket and leaves
Lighting changes | (Page 32) |

ACT I, Scene 10

To open: Street lights

| *Cue* 6 | **Fingers**: "Open up, it's Fingers and Johnny!"
Lighting comes up on the interior | (Page 33) |

| *Cue* 7 | **Fingers**: (*off*, *echoing*) I like it — I like it — I like it —
Lighting changes | (Page 37) |

ACT I, Scene 11

To open: General interior lighting

No cues

ACT I, Scene 12

To open: General interior lighting

| *Cue* 8 | **Manager**: "I suggest the best Ruby."
Black-out | (Page 44) |

ACT I, Scene 13

To open: General lighting

Cue 9   **Johnny** and **Ruby** embrace   (Page 47)
               Black-out

Cue 10   **Johnny** walks into the next scene   (Page 47)
               General lighting

ACT I, SCENE 14

To open: General interior lighting

No cues

ACT I, SCENE 15

To open: General interior lighting

Cue 11   "Today" characters stay frozen   (Page 53)
               Lights up on Ruby

Cue 12   "Today" characters freeze   (Page 54)
               Lights on Ruby

ACT II, SCENE 1

To open: General lighting

Cue 13   **Jeff** dials the number   (Page 61)
               Spotlight

ACT II, SCENE 2

To open: General lighting

No cues

ACT II, SCENE 3

To open: General lighting

No cues

ACT II, SCENE 4

To open: General interior lighting

Cue 14   **Dr Patel**: "All is calm. Calm. Calm."   (Page 72)
               Lights change

Cue 15   **Steven** turns and walks off stage   (Page 73)
                Light changes

ACT II, S<small>CENE</small> 5

To open: General interior lighting

Cue 16   **Fingers** (*off*, *echoing*) : "...at the garage... the garage..." (Page 74)
                Lights changes

Cue 17   **Steven** (off) : "...the massacre...at the garage...the   (Page 74)
                garage"
                Black-out

ACT II, S<small>CENE</small> 6

To open: Spotlight on Jeff

Cue 18   **Jeff**: "Is that idiot fiancé of yours with you?"   (Page 75)
                Spotlight on Barbara

Cue 19   **Barbara** and **Jeff** put their mobile away and step to   (Page 75)
                each other
                Lighting opens up

ACT II, S<small>CENE</small> 7

To open: General interior lighting

Cue 20   **Johnny**: "I love you, Ruby!"   (Page 81)
                Lights change

ACT II, S<small>CENE</small> 8

To open: General interior lighting

Cue 21   **Linda** and **Steven** (*singing*) : "This can't be right!" (Page 83)
                Black-out

ACT II, S<small>CENE</small> 9

To open: General lighting

No cues

ACT II, Scene 10

To open: General exterior lighting

Cue 22   **Dr Patel, Jeff, Steven and Linda** rushed off by   (Page 89)
                 policeman
                 Black-out

ACT II, Scene 11

To open: Morning. General exterior lighting

Cue 23   **Mr Pilsworth** grabs **Mrs Pilsworth**'s whisky flask and (Page 90)
                 takes a long swig
                 Black-out

ACT II, Scene 12

To open: General exterior lighting

No cues

ACT II, Scene 13

To open: General interior lighting

Cue 24   **Fingers** (*off; echoing*): "I'm in no hurry, Mr Moran"   (Page 95)
                 Lights change

ACT II, Scene 14

To open: General interior lighting

No cues

ACT II, Scene 15

To open: General lighting

Cue 25   **Full Company** (*singing*): "From moments like this   (Page 107)
                                            When the gal fin'lly kisses the guy."
                 Lights come up

Cue 26   **Johnny** and **Ruby** embrace and run off   (Page 108)
                 Lights fade out

EFFECTS PLOT

ACT I

Cue 1   Lights come up on the street   (Page 1)
Snowing

Cue 2   **Two barbers** step back in horror   (Page 2)
Shooting sound

Cue 3   **Johnny**: "... tellin' Bugs today. I'm quittin' the gang!" (Page 31)
Knocking on the door

Cue 4   **All** (*singing*): "Oh yes you've guessed the best is   (Page 54)
    yet to come!"
Loud knock on the door

ACT II

Cue 5   To begin the scene   (Page 56)
Sound of pouring rain and noisy bulldozers and diggers

Cue 6   **Mrs Clarke**: "Needs a helping hand."   (Page 63)
A car is heard to screech to a halt

Cue 7   **Mrs Clarke**: "Mr "W"! Your bloody nose!"   (Page 72)
Sound of car starting up

Cue 8   **Dr Patel**: "All is calm. Calm. Calm."   (Page 72)
Sound effects

Cue 9   **Fingers**: "Yeah Happy Valentine's Day!   (Page 77)
Sound of door banging

Cue 10   **Johnny**: "I love you, Ruby." **Johnny** and **Ruby** close   (Page 95)
    their eyes
Bangs on the door

Cue 11   **Johnny** and **Ruby**: "Ahhh!" then they open their eyes (Page 96)
Bangs on the door

Cue 12	**Bugs**: "I wouldn't bet on it, kid. Fingers!	(Page 96)
	Bang on the door	
Cue 13	**Fingers**: "Get in there!"	(Page 97)
	More banging from outside	
Cue 14	**Sergeant**: "Yeah. Ever — lovin' Al!"	(Page 98)
	Sound of fusillade of bullets	
Cue 15	**Johnny**: "Well, God must have had a hand in it somewhere...Ruby!"	(Page 99)
	Sound of approaching police siren	
Cue 16	**Johnny**: "I gave the kid my wallet! It's got everything in it!"	(Page 99)
	Sound of siren getting louder	
Cue 17	**Ruby**: "That's all we need! Come on, the window!"	(Page 99)
	Bang on the door	
Cue 18	**Johnny** push **Ruby** out	(Page 100)
	More banging	

FIREARMS AND OTHER WEAPONS USED IN THEATRE PRODUCTIONS

With regards to the rules and regulations of firearms and other weapons used in theatre productions, we recommend that you read the Entertainment Information Sheet No. 20 (Health and Safety Executive).

This information sheet is one of a series produced in consultation with the Joint Advisory Committee for Broadcasting and the Performing Arts. It gives guidance on the management of weapons that are part of a production, including firearms, replicas and deactivated weapons.

This sheet may be downloaded from: www.hse.gov.uk. Alternatively, you can contact HSE Books, P O Box 1999, Sudbury, Suffolk, CO10 2WA Tel: 01787 881165 Fax: 01787 313995.